PERTH & THE BIG SLEEP

And OTHER ESSAYS

Greg Hoey

AMAZON edition published; 2014

Publisher; ElephantProductions in alliance with 'TrashieBooks' inc.

Personal Collection of Essays on Politics both Social and Topical.

ISBN; 9781502574022

FRONT PAGE ILLUSTRATION BY THE AUTHOR

A collection of lively essays by the author about his hometown as well other areas of life, both on a social as well political front.

The Author was born in 1967 in the Gold Mining town of Kalgoorlie. A town that lies way out upon the high plains of Western Australia's vast interior plateau region.

He has three other books on Amazon; "Sydney Hideous" - "Awake I" - "Work! Work!! Work!!!

"Life it's really not meant to be taken too seriously!"

"Gamble but not foolishly, because in the end it is the gambler who will be living on the high-alter of success and admiration by his fellows!"

"Abhor all mediocrity, indeed stamp it out!!"

"TurDuckEn! What a brilliant idea!!"

"Why be a city of lights? When overhead your night sky is literally a canopy of stars"

"Is modern man afraid of the dark? Or...maybe just afraid of his own shallowness?"

"Like moth's humanity is irresistibly drawn to 'the lights, the lights'. And just like moths we are often expunged by them too!"

"Never doubt that electing some kind of Jesus figure to be sacrificed for ONE's own sweet salvation, will ever give ONE cause to be any less vain or mean-hearted than ONE already is."

Table of Contents;

Chapter1 'PERTH & THE BIG SLEEP' the definitive version. {2004-2010]

A city in isolation and the culture of complacency that can be sown from.

I rarely read the 'West Australian', unless for reasons unconnected to journalism. This newspaper has always been patronised by a readership more inclined to peruse it for its excessive classifieds section than its account of the daily news or world current affairs. The newspaper's editor whose inexperience and editorial irresponsibility /ineptitude make a mockery of politically independent & unbiased reportage, and who has a distempered somewhat circumspect disparagement of any who may not appeal to the narrow even small-minded Anglo-centric fixation he himself is given towards promoting at the expense of all else.

Although, he is not on his own. All the journalists that work in the main areas of Perth's media have an affinity for self-protection, challenge one you pretty much challenge them all. Perth's isolation can make it very prone to excessive scrutiny of any whom do not follow the jolly little white script.

It was however with despair that I observed an article written in the Saturday morning edition of this particular newspaper, where the writer seemed to be promoting the potential of the opposition leader [Barnett], to serve our state in a leadership capacity. There is in this thought the potential for concern. As for all the self-serving, self-righteous, moralising, preaching, hypocrisy of the Labor government, I worry of the alternative even more in some ways.

The opposition leader it seems is an ordinary enough bloke someone you would be quite happy to have as a member of the community or even as a decent co-member of any particular sort of recreational group etc., or even someone to just meet and greet in the street.

However, for a potential 'Premier' he is absolutely lacking in charisma, broadmindedness and imagination, and unfortunately this type of personality when placed into positions of power act exactly as ordinary normal god-fearing people would, these take their lack of imagination, their ultra-conservative values, along with their reverence for the establishment right to the top of the pole with them in their assumed roles as leaders and statesmen.

And as we have seen so many times in the past with right wing individuals as our leaders the people in the end pay hell for, [not denying all their concern for family values, why is it that whenever a potential incumbent rants on about family values when these eventually do take office they invariably are prone to creating wars, from Hitler to Mussolini, Genghis Khan and back, history is littered with self-serving demagogues that got there using the platform of family values and by kissing babies].

Indeed, it would not be wrong to suggest that this could also be said of the extremist version from the opposing political spectrum 'the Left' also. It is hard not to think of the opposition leader as being in ways a deeply conservative individual, part of the 'old guard', thanks to whom have held back Perth for so long with an ultra-orthodox Christian type mentality, which has all but ensured that Perth stays at least 20 years behind the rest of the world for most of last century, all for the misguided view that being a backwater is going to keep us all safe and out of mischief.

All this has done is that the establishment cronies have remained utterly entrenched, and that any hope of Perth being in the advanced guard as opposed to the same old rear-guard mentality is to be less an alternative than it ever was. Somehow the thought that isolation has to mean hostility to new ideas, and an overriding almost obsessive/compulsive concern for family values, as well an oppressive need for constancy, just does not sit well for many.

At times it can be difficult not to feel as though Perth is not that dissimilar to the famous David Lynch television series of the late eighties 'twin peaks'. It seems to be taking on a similarly 'darkly pretty' sort of vernacular i.e., slightly too normal not to be a little deranged, where everyone is smiley & nice and yet underneath quietly desperate, while tendering pleasant gardens under the midday sun, at the same time completely oblivious to the fact their lovely city is becoming increasingly prone to lurking violence. Nobody would doubt that Perth is not for wanting when it comes to suburban beautification. This it has in droves. But great cities have more than genteel suburbs at the heart of their makeup. Serial killers and common street stabbings now are as ubiquitous to Perth's cultural makeup as its famous golden and wide beach's. An ocean front now well and truly in the dominion of a certain set or social order of folk, far and way above the average person's wage capacity.

The dividedness based on class that this city has evolved into over recent decades is truly worrying. You have the eastern industrialized suburbs and the well-off affluent western.... Suburbs, and the twain rarely meet with repercussions that will become ever increasingly prone to disruptiveness in the future if there is not a philosophical change. A convergence of the two worlds, all types of class more closely interrelated for a more dynamic city overall.

There should be no real reason why Western Australia cannot become a modern day 21st century version

California style of state. Whereby all this backward shitty self-serving 'crony's-only' orthodoxy could not be done away with, and where instead of always being last on the ladder, Perth for all its isolation cannot become finally the place where things happen first and reverberate elsewhere, like the epicentre of a shockwave. When referring to a California style of state. I do not mean 'CALIFORNICATION' here. Just more a style of culture that yes, respects innovation and liberal progression without going loco about it. While at the same time not allowing its pragmatism to become so set and imbedded we reduce ourselves into re-action and backwardness that any creativity is abandoned and made virtually impossible.

Looking at the state of Perth's inner urban district you see skyscrapers that revel in outmoded box-like unoriginality. Simple Simon rectangularity or squared like forms that any modern metropolis elsewhere has long since evolved away from. Why is there nothing outstanding architecturally in the city of Perth? Is it because even our local government authorities are really of the view that Perth and 'Western' Australia in general are nothing more than a 'quarry state' for big mining companies with which to occupy and denude for its mineral resources? ie., Cheap and utilitarian. That's aspirational enough.

Very little value adding and very little in the way of philanthropic contributions back into the culture of the place. Being viewed as little more than a giant quarry in the outback. The only really interesting architectural statement made in the overall metropolitan area in the last 50-70 years would be the new Fremantle Maritime Museum. Really a beautiful building and undoubtedly a great entrance point into the port city of Fremantle.

But why not outsource some of the architectural work to people like the Spanish architect Santiago Calatrava, or even the American Frank Gehry. Or even Norman Foster [belatedly Sir] who in the early nineties offered freely to design a sky tower for Perth that would rival anything anywhere. The then Court government declined the offer. Perth really needs some amazing public and even private buildings with which to uplift the structural flatness of the place [witness the affect that the Sydney Opera house has had on Sydney]. A magnificent overturned pyramidal type of design standing several hundred metres into the air, whereby the higher it ascends the more width it would possess. Its structural integrity owing to massive inner supports. Somewhere down by the river perhaps? Calatrava for one would be perfect to have design a major bridge spanning across the Swan river from the Risely St., area of Applecross through & into the Crawley region where it would branch off towards Crawley's-Riverside drive as well further northwards linking with other major northern arteries.

Finally unifying the Northern and Southern precincts of the Metropolitan area. A grandly surreal and beautiful suspension bridge spanning the vast basin of the Swan river eliminating the chasm that up til now cannot be accessed unless by ocean going vessel or ferry or unless one is a fish or a bird!

 Pure. White. Practical and preferably something architecturally challenging?

An example might be of a curved taut bridge not needing to be higher above the river than any of the other existing Perth bridges, only this bridge will rely on suspension bulwark that connect and relay over each other resembling a lattice effect not unlike other major suspension bridges throughout the world but more cross woven [the way some cathedrals have suspended roofs]. Each cable lattice work descending from vast structural edifices not straight upwards but diagonally leveraged outward from each other. 3 of these would more than suffice.

Shanghai and Beijing are two cities now undertaking dramatic improvements of their cityscape that Perth administration could well take heed of. Esp., when it comes to skyscrapers and stadiums designed as dramatic and highly creative statements that reconfigure and renew their inhabitant's ideas as to themselves and their sense of place and value.

In fact, taking Perth's riverfront as an example of irrelevant old style thinking, it is a riverfront that should be at the very centre of action and for all Perth citizens, yet it seems to remain the domain of the rich and almost a closely guarded secret. Any really intelligent community would surely utilize the astonishingly beautiful Swan River as the city's main meeting place and hub, which was in fact the case in the early part of the 20th century.

Instead the Great Swan river has become a fairly isolated attraction dominated by the homes of the rich and a place that one would go to infrequently, and then usually for special occasions only, or unless one had the use of a boat, canoe, yacht or was associated with some other water sport. It has by ways always been promoted purely to be looked at from the windows of ones' car while one would drive to and from the workplace, or maybe as a great source of touristic photos. It has not been seen as a place to live necessarily unless one had won at the lottery.

Environmental overstress is a more telling example of the blinkered reactionary mentality that fails to initiate action before it is too late, because even now when it is common knowledge that our lowered rainfall is a consequence of deforestation our government and regulatory bodies still allow suburban developers carte blanche the go-ahead to build suburb after suburb almost to the very horizon.

All to satisfy the kind of redneck attitude that needs a big empty front lawn to park their 4-wheel drives upon.

Many of which are mild mannered middleclass semi-professional women between the ages of 25-40. More recently our government also opened up mineral sands mining in one of our last remaining reserves of Tuart trees. Giants as fragile as they are Monolithic. Mineral sands that once are removed were most likely the very reason such imposing sentinels grew there in the first place. This from a government claiming to care for the environment!

There well maybe a lot of balderdash in all this fashionable concern over environmental degradation and carbon pollution one hears of today, but the plain fact of the matter is that having protected and abundant forests and a closer inter-relation between human population and wildlife and the benefits this accrues is in so many major ways of its own, is enough to demand better of politicians and town planners. It is common knowledge and not in any way at all new evidence to suggest a closer relationship with the natural world is to the benefit and general well-being of all.

Sadly, it is hard not to feel that our new potential incumbent would be any more willing to deliver a better outcome for those concerned by environmental degradation or even bring about the type of change that might extend beyond the self-same old style doctrinaire this city has.... always been known for -'Over-regulated into the oblivion and....undeniably beautiful to look at but decidedly dull.'...written 20/12/04 by greg hoey.

#updated repy to mediaspy com. 30/3/05- Yes Perth has its positives and these are its beaches and probably the weather [temperate- cool wet but not aridly frozen winters, nevertheless stinking hot even humid summers] the city in its geography is undeniably pretty and in recent years has even tried to pick up the pace and catch up to the rest of the world ie., lots and lots of development going - and I highlight the east Perth redevelopment, the Subi redevelopment as examples good things happening.

But many would say it is about time too. Perth has seen its isolation as reason to be insular, dull and very closed off unless you happen to be one of the insiders. The media this way can be very, very stupid and DO NOT like their little patch in the least bit criticized. Perth's media is highly jingoistic in its orientation.

And this has also encouraged or helped create as said before 'a very insulated closed OFF culture'. The folks that work in them nearly always closely connected to each other [nepotism].

As to Perth's isolation, this could be used in a positive light and activate a kind of spark of well were at the end of the world so let's at least not let this make us complacent and as uninteresting as we can be but let our isolation make us be the most stunning iconic unique most isolated city on the planet.

It is too much as j506hn above stated quite correctly Perth is all about footy and not much else. And it does seem to attract a lot of these kind of personalities that left other places maybe because they hate interacting with others and do not much like intelligence that is not only of a sporting or beach-side culture. Perth has an apathetic consciousness. And this is why the republican issue is not what it should be here in Perth.

I too like the beachside culture also but there's got to be more than this. You have to say Alannah McTiernan & Labor do seem intent on at least trying to knock out this emphasize on smug cultural values and parochial small-mindedness. Nevertheless, she and Labor are still part of the hierarchical-value system tainted by this slack over-regulation / self-defensiveness/ 'nanny state' mentality to a certain extent.

Perth needs serious visionary work to it [Kennet like]. So much you could do to make Perth eclipse Sydney, Melbourne or wherever if they only had the guts to demand more and break with tradition and complacency. - GH.

17th jan 2006. - of recent times much has been attempted by the powers that be, to insert various little attachments around the waterfront just to show what an abundant, exciting and diverse little riverside community Perth in fact is. Such as viewing-wheels.

Typically, the Burghers of Perth have now installed down along the Perth foreshore their own version of the more famous London 'eye', only the size differentiates in the Perth version. Recognizing the potential for their city in such a honed and crisply realized fashion [however middling the vision] with the likes of this 'Wheely' thing, something that maybe similarly described as the 'Perth eye'.

In essence an object commonly seen at any small fair or country showground.

To expect different from such an administration was always way beyond the realms of possibility and 'their' imaginations. As stated before the powers that be in this city are ineptitude personified and their childish stilted tremulous little imaginations are only ever capable of realizing Perth as little more than a mineral resource/agricultural backwater.

Nothing more.

Anything inconsistent with this, such as a place of the imagination or some kind of fabulation or even some cultural relevance or depth is quite inconceivable. The end...

Welcome to Deadwood 2006.

...submitted letter to Perth city admin 12/4/09

re-the Langley lawns/supreme court lawns/esplanade lawns dead zone, down by the river. Why not just turn the whole place into a major parkland with yes 'trees' covering much of that under-utilised open area where in summer it's just too hot to warrant anything or anybody other than a few desperate birds looking for insects!

Too, too much acreage of lawn and more lawn under the hot, glare of the sun. Stupid. Hopelessly devoid of humanity. It needs beautifully landscaped gardens with waterfalls, fountains, streams, mounds, stylized contemporary replicas of archaic temples with domes & arches, columns from homage of ancient Rome, skate ramps for kids la de dah dah de etc, etc, and especially it should incorporate major Sculptural works within its boundaries- yes a 'Sculpture park' or is this just too cultured an idea for Perth City Councillor's and pollies to get their largely philistine heads around??

As well a plaza type feature extending up along barrack St., toward Hay St., purely as a pedestrian thoroughfare possibly lined by columns in recognition of a more

Mediterranean style. Riverside drive should preferably be sunk, or could be put 20-30 metres above the ground area [much like Brisbane has its expressway going beside the Brisbane river & parallel to the city] so it would not be an encumbrance to pedestrian activity, and I think an elevated riverside drive would look OK and give passing motorists good views. But really being put underground is best option undoubtedly.

In terms of an iconic structure possibly the current 'Bell tower' could become part of a much taller and larger complex of spires not unlike Gaudi's famous 'Sagrada Familia' in Barcelona ie., the now smaller bell tower staying same while much, much larger spire to the rear or as seen from Perth city the 'fore' with its base being basically a vaster more inclusive auditorium becoming even cathedral like [without all the evil religion that is] incorporating a system of walkways up to its higher perimeters in a circulatory manner so that as you walk upwards one slowly revolves their way round to the top for maximum views, reaching an open cafe area viewing platform around the whole perimeter-not unlike the Eiffel tower, however the entire height of the structure should go further to at least a thousand feet. 1000ft for main spire with other spires reaching from between 150ft [front two sp] 3-400ft [two wing spires] with bell tower at back now round 250ft mark as it is now.

Each done in stages over a period of 20 years or more. -It could also be envisioned that there would be a compliment of two medium sized twin spires to each side of and interconnected with the main central spire. These various spires would be attached at a certain height so that one could pass from one to another. As well to the front of the main spire would be two smaller spires, not unlike the way you get those two smaller shells that sit to the fore [as you go up the steps] of the main group of shells that makeup Sydney's Opera House. A magnificent, structure of masonry and stained glass. Paying homage to Gaudi in a 21st century Art Deco kind of way.

The actual buildings will be built of local stone[donnybrook] and inside will have a crystallised quality about it when gazing outwards from within with various sections over-hanging with foliage so that this will not only be a green building it will look green. This should help distinguish such a building away from being a mere simulacra of Barcelona's Sagrada Familia, bringing it into more of an original & Australian-ised architectural context.

The base as previously stated could be utilized as concert/arts activity as stated above or gathering place for special occasions Xmas etc, with the bells being rung. The ferrous wheel now there should possibly be made a permanent feature. As well the pyramid that was formerly used as green house could be again. But this time as a Butterfly-farm.

It has been proposed that residential development should be the way to go. Unfortunately, what usually results from these sort of proposals is that people with money then get hold of the whole area and it just becomes a domain of the well-heeled white shoe brigade. Although it could be foreseen that the car-park area now there might be a place of residential development. But a great and beautifully landscaped parkland/sculpture park would be inviting, peaceful and would definitely turn a dead zone into something that would breakdown and alleviate a potentially much more urbanised city of the future.

A city that renounces it's formerly staid, insular and overly conservative stance and attempts to lay claim on being one of the most advanced 'Premier' places on the globe.

postscript; 1/9/09 Unfortunately our newly elected Premier has seen fit not to undertake any fine architectural splendour for such a site, nor any such thing as botanical open aired pursuit, he much prefers Perth as a more 'down to earth' kind of city, particularly related to this riverside aspect where he would rather have more pedestrian kinds of activity be undertaken. In the shape of low level business and touristy cafes type stuff mixed up with apartments for those wealthy enough to afford them, and possibly a great cut out of the landscape with inflow of the river- with suspension bridge/overpass for the traffic just like darling harbor over in lovely Sydney town [Darling Harbor an odious & two penny dreadful tourist trap].

And unfortunately he has the collusion of our new Lord Mayor Lisa -'More Bling for Moi'- Scaffidi a woman as preposterously crass as she is woefully unimaginative. Having reached the heights of political power by way of appealing to her YOUNG & new 'visionary & female non-Anglo non old male values' point of view-except when it relates to employing foreign labor and underpaying them. [not to mention the fact she has been involved in a recent allegation/court case related to forging documents so as to gain from the inheritance of a relative] and making sure her developer husband gets in on all these lovely new inspiring visionary inner Perth developments.

Like the new up & coming Aboriginal Cultural Centre 'down by the river' proposed by our 'visionary' Premier to make it look as though he ain't a racist for bulldozing through an aboriginal sacred site only recently in the north-west mining town of Karratha.

This country now has more aboriginal cultural centres than you can poke a stick at and thousands upon thousands of aboriginals in jail and in disease. And just as serious division between rich aboriginal and poverty stricken aboriginal, as there is in the wider Australian [white] community or non-community [not that I have

19

much sympathy for a large part of the indigenous community as they have been so mischievous and self-centred over all this racial politics Australians have had to endure for the last few decades-it can be hard to really respect them at times].

postscript; 12/1/2010 -

Interesting to see a recently published book outlining a fresh, new vision for Perth. Called 'Boomtown' and authored by Richard Weller it includes the thoughts of many leading professional Perth intellectuals such as the well-known demographer Bernard Salt, our Lord Mayor Lisa Scaffidi, David Hedgecock from UWA, Simon Anderson architect, Brett Wood-Gush [architect] and other leading urban planners.

Although somewhat elitist and admittedly one or two of these people seriously worry me esp., the likes of Bernard Salt with their highly paid professional & quite superior perspectives in comparison to others. And such people can have the tendency to regard anyone less than themselves as little more than test mice in a laboratory for which these have been given the job as head splicer. Something of which all Perth's intellectual/arts high brows have in recent times been dangerously over run with.

This book does however offer a vision for Perth that maybe less environmentally corrosive and one would hope it proves more than just a pipedream. Promoting bridges across the sacred & untouchable 'swan', high-rises along our river and coastline with a much greater population taking up less indiscriminate land use in the form of low density urbanization [suburbs], better more advanced & 'creative' architecture for Perth inner city high-rise buildings can only be a good thing.

My own vision for Perth would not necessarily be for giant sized tower accommodation but rather a city much composed of suburbs not dissimilar to the outlook of West Perth's 'Mount st'., area. Or possibly of an inclination that is much more in keeping with the likes of the South Perth area, or even the regenerated domiciles of the East Perth region, [who's inhabitants seem to be of the opinion as part of the Holmes a court- 'cultural elitist mystique' that these were the ones whom invented modern Australian inner-city housing density-when in fact most early 20th century Australian federation cities and towns were literally crowded with apartment style accommodation and residential living ie., tightly-quartered precincts, busy streets that were much in denial of the greedy space cannibalising cities and suburbs of latter day Australia].

Although even Australia's premier 'city of culture' Melbourne is a city chronically ringed by miles and miles and miles of seriously bland low density housing estates. No city of culture worth its salt would ever so willingly trade-off the remnants of its verdant and lush outer urban bushland areas for the mediocre vastness of countless one-dimensional suburbs that these days almost kiss the underside of the Australian Alps. So vast and rapacious has suburban spread become in that city [Sydney is no better in this department with its western suburbs just as red-brick dreary and never-ending. Once you leave its fabulous river and coastal areas that city has to be one of the most hideously brutal looking cities anywhere on earth. It's obvious the people that designed and planned it never gave a second thought for either of those two words].

Nevertheless, if modern Perth could look much more like a composite of these three areas [esp., east Perth] it would be one of the world's most interesting and beautiful urban areas-taking on a kind of Parisian beauty. That is most of its suburbs would be made up of stylish contemporary Art Deco in format & style along with 4-8 storey in height residential apartments with tree-lined and leafy streets. There would be few mono-cultural [single storey housing

21

estates] suburbs in the new Perth and many of these unnecessary outer suburbs that have cemented over so much of our lovely native bush should be with time demolished and regenerated native forests will again take their place!

And while it is all very well for those choice people in the affluent domains of Mosman park, Floreat park, Cottesloe, Nedlands, City Beach or Swanbourne complaining about and even obstructing higher density developments in their particular areas. The plain fact of the matter is Perth is no longer a big country town of half a million people like it was in the 60's or 70's or even the 80's. These days it now has an area larger in circumference than all of Los Angeles put together but with barely a third of the population base with just as horrific traffic congestion.

And while its sister city on the American west coast has around 13 million's the population of Perth is a little over the 2.5 million mark. In fact, it's probably closer to the three million mark if you include the cities of Mandurah and Rockingham. While this is not huge it is still large enough to now consider urban development that is at least above the 3-4 storey mark. Those in the elite suburbs of Floreat park, Wembley downs, Nedlands, Peppermint grove etc., who do not agree -these need to be told in no uncertain terms to basically go live elsewhere.

WA Governments have to eventually consider the needs of all West Australian's, not only those that are lucky enough to live close to the beach, or within close proximity to jobs in the city-like those folk that pre-dominate in the convenient corridors specifically in the quadrant of uber-riche western 'burbs' that make-up the Cottesloe [and its Mayor Kevin 'the permed' Morgan], Dalkeith, Mosman Park areas which may include the vicinity of Floreat Park.

Meaning basically that property developers of the like of one David Airey, Rich Real estate, Satterly & Co, Ray White, Cockman & Co., etcetera need to be regulated.

Because although these are making fistfuls of money essentially by denuding Perth of much of its former sanctuary of native bushland/agricultural holdings that used to once surround this city. Infiltrating right through to its urban heartland and of which in the last 30 years has been basically cemented over with miles and miles of bland new outer suburban developments bringing with them it maybe said whole new infrastructure demands that the ordinary taxpayer has to pay for in the form of new roads-highways, sewage, electricity as well even more car/vehicle/petrol usage requirements.

It's easy to think that this country had massive over-population problems when you witness how many average Australians [those from the 3rd world get by in share houses several to a room] cannot under any circumstances find reasonable affordable accommodations having to resort to either camping out in their cars or on streets or be forced to submit to the demands of greedy irritating, grey-haired and ancient little landlords or their opposite those glitzy hand rubbing and be-jewelled matrons of real estate who hold you to ransom with unreasonable and excessive tenant regulation. When in fact this country with a whole continent to itself has an [official] population of barely 22-Millions!!! [unofficial population of above 35-Millions?] Preposterous situation.

Undeniably Western Australian governments of late have started to push the boundaries a bit more with the [semi-fascist] Barnett government introducing late night trading hours finally if under certain conditions and impediments to its full implementation. Also some of our architecture in the last year or so is taking on a less utilitarian-esque staidness to it and has started to become more imaginative and ambitious [Northbridge redevelopment].

In time hopefully Perth will become less of the malicious, spiteful, scrutinizing little village it has succumbed to being for far too long. So the future might be bright-who knows!

27th march 2011; alas what has become almost the high alter of Perth architectural style is this 'cool edged Minimalism' so common to many of our more modish & fashionable habitués and suburban corridors dotted and fringed along our coast line and rich river suburbs. It does not take even much of an out and out Philistine when it comes to matters architectural to find these structures rather oppressive and just plain 'functionally-ugly'.

They are homes that only the most Protestant and cool amongst us would find inviting to reside in, at least when viewing them from the outside. Owning no real sympathy toward supporting foliage or tree unless these be small easily pruned exotics [no wattles allowed in these places] and only ever allowing high design gardens & with a pure and Japanese subjugation of its natural environs altogether, these homes must consume torrents of carbon just to stay under melting point in our increasingly hot climes and just as much to stay warm in the winter months.

God help these if ever there was a carbon tax.

Minimalism to me is a style of architecture far too conveniently suited toward cheap & quick construction with absolutely no inclination to present some sort of communalism to any bar other 'insider' elites. Squared concrete slab, tile and brick is not high design to me. It is truly architecture for a time that does not in any way value humanism, just wants to overwhelm oppress or take up a fearful bunker mentality and react against it. Its brutal to the nth degree and pays homage only to a dictatorial kind of mind-set as minimalist and as clinical as the architecture that these dentists wife's choose to have built for them.

And while I'm all for higher construction along our prestige waterfront areas like Cottesloe, Leighton,

Scarborough [our coastal areas should not just be for the few, but no higher than five storeys' however]. Unless this construction is reasonably humane and friendly looking by its design and pays an element of respect to curve shape and texture as well has some residue of detail that releases a building from the purely functional, and does not only see the sacred in the brutal crisp icy whiteness of glass, concrete and steel.

I somehow doubt development along our coastline will ever win the approval of those that are more than simple-minded liberal party voting commercialists who can only ever value enterprises abrupt & impersonal over and above more sympathetic streetscape developments.

Of course all the little snipes that have jobs in that local rag 'the post' with its warlock of an editor, seem permanently attached to the view that their little 'local' blue ribbon haven of Cottesloe should forever remain sacred & untouched by any development even if it has the potential to enhance that somewhat bedraggled beach front area. That papers diametric opposite [the western suburbs news] though just as much a rag, seems to suffer from a pro-development orientation at all costs. And manned however by those of a similarly 'white bourgeoisie-feminist riven' journalistic Code/Agenda.

Oh for some fine architect to bring back a new modern form of art deco and for this style to get the backing of some government style collective. It would not be a bad thing for this city. Minimalism however that fractures the clinical severity of straight lines, breaks down the absoluteness of right angles, introduces the spherical, parades an element of the textural here and there, is not afraid of broad trees or a few bushes' -hell its fine architecture by me. Just as long as it's less imposing and bunker-like, is a little daring and might it be said possibly even 'graceful' to look at.

19th/4/11; And what a great idea to widen the footpath along Stirling highway and make this not only a one story commercial street but a 10-15 story 'commercial-residential- entertainment' precinct/boulevard with wide open tree-lined pedestrian footpaths much like those wonderful avenues European city's like Paris, Madrid, Moscow, Rome are known for! One amazing Boulevard all the way from Freo to Perth instead of the ugly streetscape it now is and has been a long time. One would severely doubt that among much of the ugly mess of this street as it is now that less than 10% of it would be worth saving for historical architectural value/heritage purposes. The rest of it all the way through from Perth city on down into Fremantle is basically cheap, nasty building design from the 1960's-70's and 80's. Dare such a thing be claimed about many other of Perth's thoroughfares and highways?

Even though, widening streets as an excuse for making them more convenient for even more motor vehicle traffic is completely unnecessary if you first provide a city with affordable night/day public transport. Seriously Day/night -7 days per week -every fifteen to thirty minutes, and watch as a couple hundred thousand people stop using their vehicles almost overnight. The old Capitalistic idea that Perth residents must be made to buy cars, pay for fuel, pay for parking tickets and parking fees everywhere as well the continual upkeep of roads and the making of new ones for all these new outer suburbs is now seen as largely an ugly outdated concept/regime that only ever really benefited a few wealthy Capitalists.-[though have to admit will wanna murder that Barnett if he industrializes and sells out to big mining interests the mighty Kimberly and all its wild beauty. So will many others.....Pastoral, Agricultural and tourism Okay. Mining off/shore or on, absolutely not!].

28/10/11-...

Constantly being harassed by the cops. Held up 45mins by them today at CHOGM, still got problems with this so-called fine that never gets cleared from my name...I've been seriously abused by one of them in a cop car who screamed at me to put my 'F'n' helmet on while cycling even though was just walking with my bike, had them on my case when some right-wing family value crank accused me of taking photos of his child with a 3mega-pixel camera at a range of over 100 feet on Leighton beach and when he called the cops proved to them that he was a freak and a crank without them offering me any sort of apology for all the muck-around, then got abused by them on their cycles in the city because they regarded me as being in their way on a pedestrian thoroughfare, then nearly got into bad argument with one of them over asking for simple directions to a pub one evening at a concert.

2/06/13- As much as one can plain dislike Barnett you also have applaud his motivations concerning Perth local suburban councils if you want this city to ever overcome its parochialism and NIMBY intolerance for diversity and difference. Our town councils are all too often pre-dominated by anti-density, white reactionary, old males and females who are very prone to elitist attitudes and NIMBY mentalities utterly intolerant to diversity or difference. And explains so much of the paranoia nanny-state family values obsession this city has always been under control of and esp. of recent times. And more especially so are our prized and sacred western suburbs!

Perth will be a truly great city with a diversity of use much of which has been normal within European society for hundreds of years. And to be quite honest a city of the like of Barcelona has more social diversity and street life vitality and vibrancy in just one or two blocks of its urban makeup than the whole of Perth put together.

Madrid and the small city of Granada even more so. if there is a dissonant chord about this lot [liberal Barnetts] it is that zoning increases must be amended so that instead of obliterate green coverage, density levels should be made so that height increases are preferred over just annihilation of any open ground which can be the outcome of moderate R zoning increases of around 50-70.

So zoning should really be taken up to around 150 if Perth wants to have density with green areas and not just be concreted into oblivion which i believe is the fundamental reason why we have reduced rainfall levels in the South-West region- too much concrete in the form of suburbanisation, not too much height density increase.

And this paranoid nanny-state obsessiveness with over-protective 'family-values' as well a deeply intolerant mind-set toward socialisation and integration of difference that has operated in this city for far too long can be explained by the way our local town councils have a 'low-density suburbs only' mania which disallows anything not confined to uniform single level housing estates. With little else about these urban areas & estates other than un-socialised youth that usually orient and seek-out their entertainment in the city at night or weekends and frequently with consequences that can be inappropriate toward a cosmopolitan lifestyle.

Our local suburbs and more especially our vast suburban fringe areas have little in terms of cultural venues, night-life, small club's & bars as well other mixed entertainment or even regular daily life like cafes, corner shops, even small to light industrial usage within these areas because this may not look wholesome or be prone to noise and activity not exclusively reserved for gardening and other sedentary protestant and neighbourly alienated behaviour.

If the Barnett Govt. is only ever remembered for being elected on lies, well this is a lie I am willing to forgive them for. Dull empty suburbs and intolerant local town councils that breed nimbyist attitudes and that hate communal-socialisation should be done away with. And really with a little technology you could programme a cheap lap-top to do everything a town Mayor supposedly is paid to do with little cost to the tax-payer other than electricity cost for running the lap-top. And a lap-top doesn't need a tea-lady either! What do these people do other than help get their crony developer mates government contracts!

Its recently been estimated that by far the largest majority of young Perth families refuse to live in anything other than a suburban single storey home with a front & backyard just like mum & dad did back in the 1960's -70's and 80's. Why does this mentality so prevail?

Because basically Perth is still an undeniably bogan city underneath the feigned/assumed cosmopolitanism. A 'neighbours' town [alike so much of Australia] where neighbours prefer their neighbours at a thoroughly even hostile distance. What's going to happen then when this city reaches a population of 5 and 6 Million's which it is headed for by the middle-half of this century? Well-designed more urbanised densities along with imaginative city and town planning incorporated with its cousin 'Architecture' can do wonderful things to the mind-set and makeup of a largely intolerant population. Making an Apartment, lifestyle not necessarily anti-pathetic toward raising normal families or even dysfunctional families for that matter.

As where such development needs to occur probably the most intelligent thing to do would be to start with Perth's outer urban areas. No new suburb should be allowed without serious density levels being taken into consideration. In fact, many of these relatively newer outer suburbs should be where really most of the higher density apartment-living & high-rise development is fully realized.

In such a way our older more historical and elegant, inner city suburban areas could possibly be saved from the plundering caused by greedy, philistine often highly ignorant real-estate developers for high-rise rental profiteering/sales. That way you kill two birds with one stone. But any home unworthy of saving and 99% of them are not, these older suburbs should too be floored and made into 4-5 storey residential apartment living with greenery retained!! Especially older trees which should be put onto a registry where if they are mature they must be incorporated into the new residential design. Also the notion that apartment living should only ever be accommodated along busy thoroughfares while only MacDonald's mansion or single storey type housing should be allowed to be built in quiet residential streets is little more than an ugly rather vicious form of class warfare.

In actual fact many of these new single family homes or MacDonald's Mansions/bunkers are often as not in fact built up to a height of four and even five storeys' in height, so what is the difference in having apartment type housing in our inner suburbs like Nedlands, Mosman Park, Cottesloe or elsewhere that is of the kind of 'burb that has only one storey housing RD-zonage.

Neither will be an outcome however when Australian politicians and political parties are allowed to receive donations from well-connected developers and similar who usually on-sell land intended for them to develop to others [on the quiet] which then forces the 'real' developer to build something cheap and tacky in order for them to realize any decent profit from their venture.

Essentially, there must be empirically based laws and regulations put into practice which imposes a certain set of building standards upon the developer that forces these to build to a certain standard. Nevertheless, while Australian political parties and local town councillors are allowed to take donations from well-connected individuals this will always be a difficult outcome to achieve. Local town councils are especially prone to this mentality. The Barnett Govt. should impose regulatory conditions into legislature for the overall good of Perth architecture and the life of the community in general.

#Though the real reason why people mostly choose to live in the outer suburbs is the comparative cheapness of doing so in comparison to inner city living where house/apartment prices are far too high. Although the cheapness of living in the outer urban areas is false economics when travel time and expenses are taken into account as well as the lack of facilities available. Foreign investors being able to buy unchecked into Australian real-estate also needs to be regulated properly, because the amount of Chinese, American, Canadian, British, Singaporean and Malaysian investment allowed into this countries home buying market is massively inflating housing/apartment prices for the average Australian home-buyer. And when these have laws regulating against foreign investment in their own countries you have to wonder why Australian government authorities so easily allow such outcomes to go unchecked!?? [corruption]. In relation to Perth's local suburban town councils being broken up and made into larger ones, I'd just like to see this little man [Barnett] do similar for state government beaurocracy as he is now doing for local councils -Do we really need State Governments? In fact, these are probably more irrelevant than insular localised town councils.

...24th march 2014;-Barnett's back to being his imperious dreamy self again.

This time with grand visions of cable cars for tourism as well as new sports stadiums. Yet the entire city is basically unliveable with rental increases absolutely astronomical and more than a thousand new residents coming here per week. [one simply cannot find anywhere in this city to rent for under $300 per week and that's cheap! And don't get me started about the price of coffee- all the Perth.

This city has now become an absolute quagmire of vehicular congestion. And all Napoleon wants to do is build stadiums and tourist facilities!! [Nothing science or high tech industry related either by the way]. -Just build more train lines Mr. Barnett and stop playing Napoleon Bonaparte unless your French is as good as his mistress Josephine's was.

Train-lines and an efficient, massive increase in public transport. Oh and while you're doing that how about fining all those people in fine houses who predominate our coastal corridors and live along our river fronts and who chop down or poison or in some way destroy trees they regard as putting an end to their beachy or river-front views at the expense of shade for the average punter.

Chapter2 American/Chinese Cultural Colonialism [2012]

In time the West will come to realize that being on the side of people like the Chinese who really want to grow and amend their poor human rights record over traditional nations like the Japanese who rely on old anachronistic ideals and outmoded terms of inter-nationalistic relations with countries like the US and its American exceptionalism sense of self-entitlement as a Christian fixated nation along with countries like Australia whose conservative branch of the political fence are too easily manipulated by Japanese goodwill into taking their side over that of the Chinese.

The West lead by the Americans need to get over their antagonism of everything Chinese [that does not mean they have to let up on them because they are still an at times brutal regime of capitalists who steal other peoples intellectual property like there is no tomorrow while trying to pretend that Chinese business is not another department of the Chinese people's party].

Nevertheless, in terms of relations I think it is the Chinese who will supersede the recalcitrance of the Japanese when it comes to race relations, cultural openness and general trade deals; -in time and with a little firm persuasion. In fact, I'll go further on the Chinese and say they are without doubt the greatest civilization there has ever been and will soon hopefully make the natural born superiority of the British, the essential arrogance of the European, and the sheer Christian, fundamentalist, lunacy and nationalist ignorance of the Americans look ludicrously out-dated and verifiably smug. Which is no doubt why the American's especially find their rise so uncomfortable to deal with? Along with with that old idea goes a more newer observation. One that sees the Chinese as extremely racially selective even somewhat inbred over the millennia. A nation, whose people have become so corrupted by a nascent xenophobia toward the outsider, that it needs to point the finger at everyone else as being 'racist.' Simply because these know full-well and acutely well at that, that this nation, this culture, this great world dragon is in fact a natural born tyrant climbing its way towards world domination largely from of others hard won ideas as well their IP. In fact, no nation has so benefitted by those foreigners it so curses and seeks to dominate, mainly as outcome of these foreigners 'laowai' having been so open to this closed-minded, intolerant group of citizens who think that what they have achieved has been an out-witting of the western foreigner? When the real truth is that much of the Chinese dragons greatest modern achievements have come from of the back of the lowly tax-paying westerner who in time will come to deeply resent this usage stemming from much goodwill.

A very good reason why the teaching of Mandarin should be at the forefront of Australia's school curriculum. We need to meet this new/old civilizational power head-on, if we want to come out of it with our pants on and not beneath our knees.

The Europeans, British and the Americans are in fact living in a hazy, somnolent, dream based on old glories. This is a chance for dumb Australia to rise and not remain colonials at the ass-end of the world like we have done for much of our history. If I have any qualms with the Chinese mentality, it is their culture of "Work! Work!! Work!!! Money! Money!! Money!!! -Then you die." This attitude in fact, over-rides the rest of oriental Asia have made them into an unquestioning Slavic mass. The Chinese population have tended to have been bred by their superiors with which to uphold robotic-like attitudes/traditions which relate somewhat toward their own and everyone else's individual freedoms. This aspect of their culture worries me.

Yes, Australians can be fairly gauche in their very strident and excessively exuberant cultural leanings, but individual freedom used to mean something here. With incremental asianisation of the West [including Australia], along with 'free-trade' over the last four and five decades this has to quite an extent helped undermine individual freedoms and aided in making us as conditioned to authority and thus far more easily manipulated by our new Mandarins [free-trade orientated political leadership] along with this Buddhist philosophy of peace and harmony and absolutely NO toleration for criticism or critical dialogue;- just consume like good, little, thoughtless, robots do -like the Chinese and Japanese do!

And recently the Indonesian Consular General in my home town of Perth, Western Australia have put it out that Australia could become a nation like so many others throughout Asian and the US and Europe who rely on imported indentured labour from countries like Indonesia to work as nannies and for home-care services and things of that sort.

I think this would be quite appealing to a new and modern Australian with its emphasis on the Nanny-state and nice, large houses for the nouveau riche [many of whom are not inter-generational Australians many are of course Singaporean, South African, English, Chinese as well as the more conservative avuncular racist right-wing capitalist rich Anglo-aussie]. When in fact this is just one short step away from slave-labour and having been hounded throughout the nineties as being somewhat of a whinger for my views on the way the business community and many of these Labour Hire Firms [who were often as not owned by British companies and who had a real antithesis toward employing Australian's it seemed].

I think this is just another continuance of that same mentality. Where some are allowed to have high-paying working conditions and others are considered expendable and it's surprising how so many soft left liberals who are so concerned about refugee's and the rights of gays are not in the slightest concerned for their fellow Australian on the ever decreasing median wage! Many of these liberals do have life time positions as well high profile jobs as journalists at the Australian Broadcasting Commission or otherwise roles in various liberal leftist journals, magazines or blogs.

I'm sure our new PM will be a supporter of such an idea from our Indonesian friends but in the main I think this is continuing down a very rocky slope. Many people both Australian born and immigrant [quite often as not it can be those from war-torn countries with little in the way of freedom or human rights] like to devalue Australians as a bunch of racist lazy bludgers [again true for some-certain librarian staff for example, management, politicians, some trades, many highly paid professionals and certain bureaucrat's] who get paid far too much for doing way too little [and we even have Medicare and social security payments-how dreadful!!] and this appeals to a certain mentality within Australia who don't mind themselves being paid quite well in comparison to others but these can then openly voice displeasure when the lowest waged and often un-unionised get a pay rise, even by the slightest!

But I think what so many people particularly those in the US, Canada, Britain, France and throughout Europe and Asia and other parts of the 3rd World should recognize, is that it is not an especially bad thing to have a well-paid working-class population with good work conditions. Because this has a positive effect on putting back into the society in which these conditions came from. When you just have a few fabulously rich folks at the top these have a tendency to want to avoid the upkeep of their own nation. Not seemingly being able to recognize the fact their nations business and work regulations probably contributed mostly to 'their' being able to rise above the pack in the first place.

I would not like to see Australia's median wage go the way of countries like the US where to make a reasonable living someone in the services or hospitality industry must hope for tips in order to make a decent wage. But there are those that would mark us as inferior for wanting to remain as we are and not become like the US. These type of people would deride Australians as being stupid, racist, dumb-convicts living under a Nanny-state sadly, which I think has truths for some but is definitely misplaced for the entirety. And it would be sad for a nation that was the first in the world to institute things like workers' unions and regulation wages as well as the first 8hr day for the worker, to renounce such values and become as slavish and disordered as so many other western nations [who consider us slightly inferior with our convict related past] to go down!

Chapter3 A Great Southern Republic [2013]

We have just witnessed in this past week a very nice young couple who have had the uncommon decency to pay the colonies a visit, and who from all appearance seem to be genuinely in love with each other, even taking into consideration all the agenda-centred politics that might be festering around such an honest commitment to themselves and their lovable, new baby young George.

By politics I'm referring to the political machinations that may see such a love-story as potentially great material with which to persuade Australians and other nations that remaining relegated and colonised to another nation's historical, formerly grand and glorious past will somehow be svelte, ideal, even sexy for us, & basically good for us. And what a beautiful, 'young', potential pair of Monarchs we may be fortunate to share sometime in the not too distant future if we play our cards right and be good, abiding, loyal little colonials under a southern sun [we might also get to have the very cute 'Baby George' too, as a potential Monarch sometime in the year 2190 if we're still that emasculated and dumbed-down enough?].

The spoilers of this Royal Parade however are those terrible, pant-less but kilted, bag-pipe, playing antagonists the Scots [and I'm not talking here of those pretend 'english born and bred-scots' who try to make out how Scotland becoming a Republic will be a www-eally, w-weally bad thing because the earth might somehow suddenly start spinning extra, extra fast and it might even lose control and there's no telling what might happen after that!! The Sun might explode, Mars may fester and Uranus may turn into one gigantic, over-sized, space-bag of inter-galactic cow-dung].

No it's the bloody pain in the bum Scots who are seemingly determined to unravel and challenge the myth of the British [English] Empire with all of its historical baggage, by seeking of their own sovereignty and true national independence? Something so many Australians sought for their own subordinated nation back in the year 1998.

And from an Australian perspective our referendum on the Republic in 1998 was one in which the impetus for becoming a republic was seen to be massively in favour [at least 80% for becoming a republic] over remaining merely a somewhat inferior contributor to the English and their misplaced 'sense of nationalist superiority' over their rather elemental colonies, something which in many respects has long since departed them.

Unfortunately, at that time [1998] we had John Howard as our PM, who had quite a fierce mania for his Anglophile roots as well a need to prostrate himself and his fellow countrymen into mere British boot-lickers. He along with an imposter on the Labor Party side, one Kim Beazley both articulated the argument so that this 80% majority had no other option other than to vote with the Tory's and the British aristocracy's continued bludging off of the country.

Essentially they framed the question into "Do you want to remain with the Queen of England?' or "Would you prefer an AMERICAN style republic where only politicians are allowed to vote their President in?!!"

-proved disastrous as it was meant to by the passionate Anglo-Phile minority desperately opposed to us becoming a Republic. It's good to see Scotland's attempts at becoming its own man so to speak has been much more direct in asking similar questions as to its own attempts at abandoning this ancient and somewhat anachronistic, even parasitic relic of the past, maybe they learnt from us?

However, is it not time for the English to come to the realization that the empire has long since set? And acting as though they still rule the high-seas is plain annoying but also something they just cannot seem to overcome and break free of. Ultimately nations like Scotland or Australia [or even New Zealand which is also now seeking to have its own flag, hopefully it will be the beautiful, silver-fern on black background] growing-up and finding their own way with their own sense of statehood will be as good for the English as it will be for all its inherently, inferior colonials? That is to walk a different but not completely separate path away from being subverted by an English

'Head of State' that is defined largely as over and above everyone else solely by virtue of birth-right, in this Commonwealth of Nations, something that is basically at its heart little more than a symbol of inherent class bigotry and inculcated, hereditary racism.

Something as much suffered by the English themselves as 'the colonies'. Basically saddling all, in this Commonwealth of Nations with.

What can be truly disheartening is witnessing our common superiors [your typical public transport utilizing Englishman/woman] a certain percentage of who happen to be class brutalized, excessively nationalist, lager-louts who without much thought will openly defend the honour of something which they believe [by way of a combination of ignorance or brain-washing], gives to themselves and the nation of the English some kind of cultural superiority & glamour over all others, but which has in reality been constructed in order to keep such folk in a semi-permanent state of real class subservience.

When the 'colonies' like Australia or Scotland realize they are not inferior either culturally or economically and finally rid themselves of this symbol of national subservience [which confines them into ugly class and cultural stereotype's which often result in being seen as little more than English proxy's which does huge damage to their own relations with other nations not of the 'Anglo-sphere', as well an inferior sense of their own capabilities] this will give the English lower/working classes whether white/black/Asiatic as much freedom from their class consignment/yolk as it will give to all the 'colonies'.

This does not mean that all relationship with our British cousins must come to a sudden conclusion [we should and could never deny that our essential origins are necessarily of British stock], it just means that when their Monarch if they happen to retain such an institution into the future, when such a monarch does care to pay us a visit they shall come here as equals to our own self-realized Head of State. That includes the common Englishman and woman too, not just their Aristocracy.

Because the fact is those rather jingoistic Australians who gallantly clothe themselves in our flag while crying out for "NO CHANGE to either our constitution or our flag" really only care for the Monarch of England out of self-interest, because this confirms to their minds how these are racially and culturally the true and official brand of any Australian identity-full stop. When in reality they don't really take either the 'English Royals' or the English themselves that seriously, often deriding anything English and even being highly antagonistic to Englishness in all truth.

One only has to look to the world of sporting competition to confirm this. -'Pure unadulterated hatred' is not that far off the mark and is often registered by both nations toward the other. In fact, the English are much more inclined to take such things to heart than an Australian would. And sadly no Australian has ever witnessed an English Royal barrack for us in sporting competition, being much more inclined to want to jump up and down from joy whenever an Australian even looks like being beaten, especially if it happens to be by an English competitor.

And for those English who prefer to reside here and not England and yet stridently demand we remain loyal to a 'Christian and English identity and none other and NEVER, EVER change the flag!!' the reality is they are often highly contemptible of 'lowly white Anglo-Australia' whom they class as being essentially derived of convict stock and irredeemably so.

 The sad reality is our English friends including the Royal Family really only desire our loyalty to them because of the prestige this imbues to their now rather lacklustre and insignificant nation in terms of its former standing on the world stage especially when face to face with much more formidable euro nations such as the Germans.

Without countries like Australia or Scotland in cultural submission to Mother England our English superiors would no longer be Great Britain they would practically disappear into the mass of Europe and just be seen as a middling, far less significant power in the EEU and the world in general. More a 'Little England' instead of a "Great Britain" if you like.

Other than that the English and their Royals could give a damn about Australian's or even Scotland for that matter, although I somehow suspect that of all the colonies it is Australia they regard as the lowest simply because of our origins –Hell! even the average parochial New Zealander considers us beneath them.

So Australia becoming a Republic will be good for us because we will no longer be under the comfortable allusion that Mother England is safely at hand even when experience has shown to us differently-because 'M' England in actual fact prefers to run when her colonies are in danger of being invaded by hostile forces, she's only there for the good times rarely for the hard times as are most colonisers and we might also start to register more creativity about this nation of ours -more manufacturing/industrial prowess? And be less stupid, dumb, rock exporters with mindsets overly-assured about our racial origins.

An important outcome of this might also be less class snobbery something that now has taken hold of so much of this countries cultural & intellectual elites often parading as higher political & ethical virtues and the often rather dreadful, quite obvious nepotism associated with these areas of our social life enveloping these areas safely out of the hands of those disconnected from the upper-middle classes. Where such 'professional conclaves of intellectual elites' have for far too long now prevailed, and where if one is not born of that realm you get the feeling that the message is 'do not waste your time, or mine unless you have appropriate connections. Just look at what has happened to the ABC and the BBC in the last decade or three.

In terms of this the English too may start to finally have to reappraise themselves as being a little less superior because of their former historical success as a once great militaristic, economic and colonising power, and as stated before they may start to question an ugly entrenched, class system which allows their Aristocratic class to seek a seat in the English Parliament without having to do so by merit. And is the sort of thing that inculcates huge damage and very, unhealthy attitudes to the nature and values of your average Englishmen/women in terms of how they see their place in the world.

Basically the English need to re-define and remake of themselves & their society as much as any nation, as much as any Commonwealth nation needs to do. And one way they will renew and invigorate themselves is to finish with an abhorrent class system and finally come to the conclusion that Britannia no longer rules the globe 'from where the sun rises, till where ever it happens to set'.

# of recent times our version of the English Tories 'the liberal party under Tony Abbott have been remarkably adept at doing everything and anything to make Australia compliant and safely dumbed down in order to keep us nice and safe from ever escaping the cultural shackles of being lesser Englishmen. And they have striven to achieve this by bringing in absurd Knighthoods of Empire something as out-dated as stone-age wheels for a Lamborghini, detonating anything about the country that is not to be equated with dumb simplism's.

Like for example the annihilation of our motor vehicle manufacturing industry usually run ragged under the helmsman-ship of either Americans, South Africans or anyone other than an Australian CEO it seems?

Almost as soon as English born and educated PM Tony Abbott's Liberals took office they basically threw hundreds of thousands of Australians into unemployment cues, targeting people on low incomes and demanding their budgets be cut substantially all the while bringing in huge child-care subsidies for the rich while complaining about how we are living too high on the hog [which admittedly many are] and then cutting just about anything for the average Australian because of supposed massive budgetary deficits created by the incompetence of the Labor party. Also in typical Tony Abbott dumbing down of Australia form his government has no minister for science? They have now funded a visit from the Royals [how much did such a thing cost the lowly tax-payer] and only recently have ordering from the American's $24 billion dollar's, worth of jet-fighters for just one sector of our military alone!

Many Australian are now asking how all of this budgetary constraint adds up when they are spending like caftaned sheiks in a whore-house on the one hand and on the other forcing the nation into further subservience to 'M' England?

One could ask of our new PM by all means we must have a military because war is probably just around the corner but stop continuing on with the tradition of dumbing down this country for the benefit of others Mr. Prime Minister please, because this country needs to go beyond the mindless?

Chapter4 ANZAC Day's Long Shadow [2014]

Does this country need to change the focus it presently seems to have concerning its Anzac legend?

Many people think that Australia celebrates our war history very much with blinkers on, meaning has this nations war remembrances been taken over far too much by an almost theological /sacrificial /redemption complex? Where our ANZAC's are being used by basically somewhat sclerotic, recalcitrant old traditionalist's with which to promote a really quite evil, even slightly insane religious doctrine through our military history.

A mentality well passed its use-by date. A mentality that keeps Australians well and truly under the 'loser is best option' where we keep sending men into foreign wars to basically be misused all for the good of foreign monarchs and foreign governments to ultimately serve best the interests of others. Where we are regarded as little more than good and grateful to die for 'Queen & Empire' -and anyone else for that matter, little unquestioning tin-soldiers. This is the message we typically keep getting told via some of the mindsets who run the RSL. i.e., "Gallipoli was a fine disaster we should never try to expand upon" and so this pattern for our nation is well set.

But really if this country wanted to celebrate its military history then surely one of the bravest battles we have ever been utilised for actually served our own interests, not some foreign governments.

No.1 off the block would have to be what a bunch of poorly trained, largely unprofessional, conscripted soldiery achieved on the Kokoda Track in World War II. Turning the whole tide of the Pacific theatre of war on its head against massive Japanese opposition no less, while most of our more professional forces were being well used by Churchill and the British in their closer to home European campaigns even if this was against the desperate, hopes and desire of most Australian civilians, including our own war time Prime Minister John Curtin. It was Kokoda that embarrassed the Americans into the firm realisation that they needed to act with much more focus.

It was men as this that were our true surviving, winning hero's and they were not just used as shrapnel fodder 10,000 miles away from their own familiar homeland usually in some insensible, geriatric, ill-conceived military manoeuver for the amusement of a bunch of witless, stupid, befuddled, nepotistic, aristocrats sitting around in their tents made dumb-struck and incoherent by way of expensive whiskey and cigars their rich uncles and aunts sent them to help 'pep' them up if things got a little stiff on the war front.

Or maybe we could focus on another lesser known battle front where we actually kicked-asse 'big time' and didn't just die like good little dogs for the English. I am talking of what is considered possibly the greatest light-horse charge in military history "The charge of Beersheba" in World War 1, which was an epic success story for the Australian military and not just a humbled sacrifice/slaughter fest. And where we stole Palestine away from out of the clutches of the Turk's with amazing style and heroism [sadly the effects of this bold, valiant military achievement has had a distinctly bad outcome for the Palestinian's over the decades].

The Australian forces lost only four men and few if any of our great and even braver military horses!!

Sadly, the horses did in the end have to be put down because the British Commanders refused to allow the Australians to bring them back home, demanding they be handed over to the cruel ministrations of the local population who would have only mistreated or plain butchered such loyal & brave animals.

Other conflicts could also be used as fine examples of our military history where failure was not the only option to be expressed or celebrated. Conflicts like the Korean civil war, or The Vietnamese War where Australian Forces often fought in some of the most famous battles there and showed of themselves to be some of the finest soldiers a nation could have. Then there are those current engagements throughout the Mid-East and Afghanistan. Battle-fronts that have been all but excluded from being rightful acknowledged by those who control the RSL.

Why then does the old boy Anglo-Saxon network of the RSL not make such stories of victory its main focus?

Because basically I sense the focus on Gallipoli is a cunning way in which the interests of religion and race are served using ANZAC Day as a platform in which to maintain ugly, stupid, racist, Anglo-centric, mythological and sacrificial jingoism on behalf of the elite few. And where historical tragedy is okay if it in a way upholds racist traditions and ideas, but if the history is proven to be in ways negatively inclined toward such white Christian iconography then this must be erased from our memories?

Subtle Anglo-Saxon Christian icons served up on our plates to us like the lesser, gullible, colonial, piss-ants they inherently register the people of this nation to ultimately be. We need to move on in terms of ANZAC celebration and not let such tragic histories makes us servile and available for even further usage in future conflicts where our role is only to be ugly, bloody, expendable and disastrous.

Chapter5 JAPAN AND WHALING [first written in 2002]

Recently the Japanese have been exposed as the world's worst over-fishing predators in terms of their tuna catch not being compliant to signatory obligations pertaining to the world fishing regulatory council, in that they have been allowing over the last twenty years an unrepresentative figure far and above what they should be importing into japan.

And this has largely been disguised and allowed to go ahead by western nations in full compliance. Why?

The Japanese have now eclipsed America as the world's leading car maker and exporter. Even within America itself, Japanese brands rule what people buy. Interesting? Within the very nation that identifies freedom and liberty largely through the car, of which much of Americas nationalism revolves round, Ford, G. M. Holden, as well other brands. Now relegated as inferior brands to Toyota, Honda, Suzuki and others.

No doubt the Japanese make better more reliable cars. But are there other reasons?

Some may say that the Japanese have far less barriers to doing business in the west than they give to outsiders that may seek to do business in japan. For instance, American car-makers must pay into retirement funds and other for their workers that Japanese car manufacturers even though these maybe based within the u.s. are not obligated to do. Even more recently we have had symbolic world remembrance for what happened to them in WWII, with large gatherings of people in various cities uniting along with various Japanese to speak for peace and 'no more nuclear' banners being held high etc.

Nothing of what the Japanese did from that time...Things to be remembered, things to be forgotten.

Millions of Chinese put to death, as well other south-east Asian people's, thousands of enslaved British soldiers, many carpet bombed and bloodied cities and states throughout the pacific region [oddly hushed up to preserve Japanese-Aust trade relations is the fact most Australian cities were at times heavily targeted. Japanese air and naval operations bombed many of the towns/cities from Sydney to Darwin to Perth].

The recent news of how the Japanese have breached for the last twenty years their fishing obligations to the near extinction of various blue-fin and northern pacific tuna comes as no surprise, but the fact that non-Japanese and largely western nations like the Australians have known all along yet have allowed them to so easily get away with it is really worrying.

The Japanese have one of the largest armies anywhere in the world next to the Americans. They are increasingly pursuing a more aggressive component of their 'self-defence' force. With the pretext explained as not being able to be of real useful help as part of western peace initiatives. Ie, they want to be able to shoot to kill rather than just be peaceful and used in ways only related to low warfare areas.

Something about their concerns just does not ring true. Like their allegations that they have to 'slaughter whales for scientific purposes in order to save them as a species', with the result all this slaughtered meat ends up on the tables of Japanese restaurants, not in scientific labs. with ongoing propaganda from the Japanese Government trying to push whale meat as Japanese tradition and a true Japanese should be tempted to indulge such tradition.

Whaling 'tradition' for the Japanese was always a very limited proposition 200-300 years ago in that it was largely limited to a few regions in northern japan that fished for them in local water regions and not in industrial strength numbers for Japanese everywhere.

Their culture is still deeply homogenous; some might suggest still as insular/inbred as what they were prior to being forced into compliant American capitalism as an aftermath of WW11.

Some might suggest that the Japanese have attained capitalist perfection, if one regards the common exercise of dying on the job and remaining in such a preserved state for a number of days before the realization has finally arrived that the time of one's retirement has been declared. Not uncommon within Japanese society, in fact it's quite a trait.

For all the success the Americans had in getting japan to be a good little capitalist country, baseball is even the national game, not karate or sumo wrestling or even origami. One cannot help feel that this success only accords to American determination after the world war to make the world in its own image, and in the case of japan this has been effective only so far.

OK so they can be cute little copyists and nicely co-operative in terms of seeming like a democracy in line with US Westernised thinking of what capitalist/democracy is, but looking at the heart of japan and what it has turned into I think you'll find a pretty sick puppy. Immoral and desperately devoid of substance in comparison to what the Japanese culture may once have been prior to modern westernization/industrialization.

Much of their shallowness has been the result of westernised forgetting or face turning because this was good for the new world order, unbridled free trade with democracy a second thought.

In the case of the Japanese this is going to come back and haunt us, especially the US and other pacific nations. They have been allowed to much of a free for all because the west needed allies against non-free market nations, and now that global capitalism rules where democracy has been an after-thought and America is being surely usurped from its dominant position, the Japanese will in the end play by their own rules. We in the west have allowed the Japanese a clear getaway in terms of them being truly democratic and principled about where they are going with what we have forced of them, and what they intend doing when they arrive. And they do want to dominate the pacific rim make no doubt of that, like they have always seen of themselves the racially genetic cultural supremacists of the world that nearly pulled of a world coup' only 50 or so years ago. They are back.

Or very nearly and with the aid of the very people that fought for their dear lives in order to see themselves not to be an enslaved people. The men/women that sacrificed their lives from that time must surely be turning over in their graves if they could watch this whole exercise in Japanese-US [allies] relations and the way its unfurling. It's fairly disgraceful really.

With the Japanese one can no longer allow them to be so easily forgetful of things that they need to remember. To hell with unbridled free trade if it demands of people that such things can be so easily dismissed as not significant, or where principles are allowed to be made light of if it means shares to be bought and sold must be the only basis for modern democracy.

In the case of japan it must be demanded of them that they comply with fishing treaty's and fines should be enforced, if not by the proper bodies there has to be trade sanctions, and they must not be allowed to become proactive in terms of their military unless they abide and refrain from whaling.

The military should be used in order to enforce of them a whaling ban. The trade compact of which the Japanese are the clear winners using cultural specific reasons for not opening up fully to other nations exports (as well compliant western regret over Hiroshima) need to be revised as no longer should they be able to have closed markets in terms of agricultural, racial other areas. Education system must be able to identify the role of the Japanese in ww2 as clearly an aggressor.

But with the Japanese now is the time to act not tomorrow.

-Postscript 11/12/09 with the Rudd government and particularly our environment minister peter garret having come in to government with one of their major platforms being to "stop Japanese whaling", its not at all amusing to see how quickly these have capitulated to Japanese recalcitrance in their intentions to remain as a modern first world whale slaughtering culture.

Having come out today and publicly announced to the world quite openly 'how these will continue to hunt in Australian oceans and beyond' whether Australians like it or not! Using the same silly old argument of how this is all for science along with the retort -'you Australians put kangaroo on the barbie' so there.

Blunt. Recalcitrant. No room for compromise at all there and the weak Rudd government just lays down upon their backs and thinks of England. Amazing. This kind of recalcitrance defies all the characteristics of what many perceive the reality of true Japanese cultural riches to be. That is a culture that could be described as being one of the most highly developed, refined and utterly focused upon and inspired by nature. Although an undeniable aspect to this is a culture also that is maybe overly attached toward making nature servile and compliant as beautiful and honed as this imagination can often be [Japanese sculptors/artisans like Toshio Lezumi, Keizo Ushio, Koichi Ishino are definitely world's best practice though].

The Japanese are desperate for Australian Gas and Iron Ore in order to sell these back to us in the form of cars and other high technology having done this now for more than fifty years even belying the fact that Australia has other major markets for these resources. And this government cannot get some backbone to use this fact to in some way announce back to the Japanese that this market and all its advantages of being open and freely available to the Japanese will be shut until they dis-continue with coming down to Whale in the Southern Ocean.

In time the Japanese will realize that Australia has always been a very open and easily accessible economic market place for them as well a loyal ally and in good time this openness will be missed and their whaling income will be seen for what it is. Trivial and little more than a side dish in terms of viable economic pursuit or so-called 'tradition' especially if it is going to affect their relations with such a stable and ready ally as Australia. -And this ally did not ban whaling back in 1978 just so the Japanese could take up where we left off.

...; postscript 16th may 2011;

Some months ago the world bore witness to giant rolling tsunami's breaching landfall and literally pounding japans nuclear power stations into submission. And again the world opened up its heart and elicited despair & consolation.

And again the Japanese get a let off as they so often have throughout the 20th century and it seems this new one as well. Few saw fit to ask why did they build their nuclear energy sites so catastrophically close to an earthquake zone, and along coastal flats so close to major cities. Allowing them to become hazardously unregulated & technologically out-dated, with scant thought for a back-up plan in the case of a major crisis such as this?

And few if any dare harangues them over the vast amounts of nuclear waste that has resulted from this episode to be spewed out into an Ocean we all share and survive from. Another sign of a nation with little 'leftist' or even centrist opposition. Only what is patently a right-wing corrupt xenophobic nationalist orientated Government.

Chapter6 Now that the Japanese have been stopped from Whaling? {2013]

Now it might be time to instead of being seen for hypocrites Australian's should also start to question the live cattle and sheep trade which set up against the whaling business makes the cruelty of Japanese Whaling look quite innocuous by comparison! Because the live cattle and sheep trade into the middle-east, Indonesia and elsewhere is brutal beyond all imagination. Particularly for a so-called white, progressive, middle-class first-world nation like Australia. Our farmers need to literally take stock and not be so persuaded by the easy profits of condemning animals into inhumane, non-ritualized barbarism. They are no longer the main stay of this country and should no longer be allowed to pre-dominate over country and city by way of unchallenged farming traditions and privileges.

We must also begin to question the practices of our own indigenous native peoples too with their own kinds of horrific animal carnage these are allowed to practice under the policy of 'native integrity for the noble savage'.

Sadly, the sort of thing being practised upon much of our native wildlife by Australia's first peoples in various tribal communities is just that -ugly, backward, stone-age animal cruelty coming from peoples whom are at least within the top 5% in many cases when it comes to Australia's richest, most well educated sector. They are no longer stone-age or pre-industrial age they now are very much integrated into modern post-industrial society as Lawyers, Doctors, Artists, Writers, Musicians, highly paid Athletes, Scientists, Educators, Media personalities, Actors, Miners, Tradesmen/Women, Bankers, Bakers, Ballet Dancers, Politicians, Academics. Unless they choose not to be.

It's time for them to also instead of just berate others but to take responsibility for their own attitudes and practices toward Australia's animal wild-life, not just with words or ceremony but through practice.

#One of my earliest memories relate to the year of 1971-72 where as a small child I happened to watch on the recently introduced Kalgoorlie television service a piece about the new sport of big time surfing on the island of Maui and the gigantic waves and wipe-outs which various surfers undertook, and included along with this focus on world water adventures was some very disturbing footage of the way the Japanese lured dolphins into a bay in the small town of Taichi whereby they basically hacked them into bloody slaughter with knifes. It was some amazing footage to witness at that time and surely if there is a case for whales to be saved from Japanese butchery then one could just as easily make such a case against this fairly brutal practice too perhaps?

Chapter7 Julia Gillard; party machine fembot? Updated

3/8/10- I cannot help but think that without all the Labor party machine men behind this one, she would never have ascended to the heights we know her of today. She is an example of a woman used to being carried throughout her life by the complacency and fashion of feminism, of witch I refer to in my essay 'if woman ruled the world'.

She has neither high intelligence, nor even a reasonable type of statuesque beauty with which one could use in order to discover more about her than there really is.

Beauty definitely has its advantages as more than just eye candy. And that dull monotone voice only clarifies the complete lack of vision related to her wanting another term as our PM. The way it seems to chant -Elect me!...elect me!...Not because I have much more to offer, but because I'm a woman! How about coming up with some policies that excite people you dull feeble-voiced drone-on.

The opposition's new visionary platforms are not much better but they're conservatives, it's what one expects. They govern for rich old White guys/women that want the status quo preserved.

And with all the zillions the conservatives have by way of support to basically keep Australia in a low state of manufacturing and skill capability as well wage level ie., being able to call upon not only Australia's rich billionaires but more importantly having a fundamental support network coming from what Tony Abbott terms 'the Anglo-Sphere' ie., high born Protestantism like those rich aristocratic investors throughout the united kingdom, the US, Europe and even Japan that run Australia by proxy through the liberals,-then the only way you can dislodge or keep them from gaining power is by running on a platform of real Structural Innovation & Civil and Technological progress and Reform as well true and charismatic Leadership potential.

I would like to know one thing however concerning male patriarchy and this is when has the female ever originated and advanced her own large scale industry or big business? Rarely. There have been one or two in the fashion/perfumery business [Coco Channel], but other than this all man-kinds great industrial and big business or infrastructural attainments were largely off the back of the male animal. Eventually through bad marriage or from what we currently term Gender Equality the female may have acquired helmsman ship of an enterprise over and above her male counterparts or maybe through bequeathal had been left the business of her father who was perhaps a successful entrepreneur.

Essentially if females want to run big business they need to start creating their own. -[Of course we all know of those decent and forgiving females that can tend to fall in with all the theoretical good will and cunning of sanctimonious, charismatic and often bullying males, only to then be used & dropped when these fondly seek a life elsewhere].

Gillard's attempts at being clever by asking Abbott for another debate, when barely one week ago she point blankly refused him anymore debates -because polls showed she looked like being elected, only goes to show what a simpleton she really is. A serious, deep, dark and dull heavily, complacent, simpleton.

Miss Gillard is no 'robot', alack alas, -she with her dronish voice and with that repetitive 'going forward' catch phrase the Labor party seem to have supplied her with from deep down within the tired old and out-dated bowels of the Labor party dungeon, - does definitely remind one of a 'Zombie' though.

And a Zombie without any vision just as you'd expect one not to have.

And like all good Zombies- they're want is to backstab and feed succubus-like from off the good work of others whose corpses like Rudd's lay isolated and alone in their swirling misty and discombobulated chambers. Their recently dismembered presumably dead rag of a body slowly arising on its almost certain trail of vengeance destruction and blood.

Leaking to the left of it and more importantly leaking to the right of it.

Roaming the corridors of Parliament and assailing any members of the ALP the 'K-Rudd' zombie can lock its fleshy corpuscular ruination of a once fine aperture of a mouth onto.

With various elements of the Labor party going down like gutted ferrets in a cage less fox farm it was only through the cunning enticement of a young female staffer, herself having recently experienced being mauled by a prominent member of Parliament [let's call this a passage of career opportunity, while at the same time being a demonising feminist when the circumstances suited her] who by opening a door, persuaded the K-Rudd Zombie to venture forth into the eternal delight of the Senate where many fine figures of politic were awaiting to have his gangrenous lips and wasted teeth sunk into their necks, backs, bellies and swarthy tit.

Where on entering she slammed the door shut on the K-Rudd Zombie to the considerable applause of all her fellows. It turned out to be the mop and bucket room and only a mournful clanging and banging about could be heard coming from the inside. This was a corpse that no longer cared for all the pretence and falsity of keeping up appearances. With little concern anymore for the Labor party look of 'Political Correctness' that presumes all women are bound to one day be leadership material whether brainy and charismatic or not. Some personality or nil.

Zombie?

Or just the puppet of Machine Men, with little ideas themselves that may relate to making this country really great.

That will no doubt be decided in the coming election by the voters of Australia. Moving forward -moving forward-moving forward- moving forward....te...dium te...dium.

postscript 8/8/10;- The more I see of this dread-eyed zombie 'Julia Gillard' and her fellow neutered little boyish looking colleagues such as Penny Wong, Kate Ellis, Paul Howes, etc etc. the more i worry for this country. She rarely gets any real tough questions asked by all the predominately female journalists that are in the Australian journalistic profession these days and is now so used to just dishing out spin and rhetoric, in full knowledge of the pathetically soft line that will be taken with her, with little to no comeback from all the fellow girl luvvies.

The fact is this government of which Gillard has been a mainstay has constantly stuffed up with their pink bat scheme, their school hall scheme, the Ken Henry Tax reforms, the so-called Great Rudd ideas initiative that has been largely waste-binned, and now so I fear will they stuff up on their new Broadband Network and their policy of fixing the Murray-Darling with their water buy back scheme, -as they most likely will with regards boat people too.

They claim they've managed Australia out of a world recession when in fact it was selling off resources to China that managed us out of the world recession. They are in-competent fools that have only incompetence, in abundance to their glittery little pink purses [of the public's money] and little else other than high-minded rhetoric. They need to be done with and quickly.

Their constant high-minded rhetoric's are little more than unachievable and largely impractical and the sooner- their 'luvvies' in the media catch onto them and give them more of a hard time and not allow her and her mates to just excuse themselves and parry a hard question from one minister to another and even attempt to just walk away from camera scrutiny [like I saw this morning at a conference in Adelaide] when a question becomes altogether too tough and not controllable, over what are extremely complacent and little scrutinised agendas about them being returned to high office,-the better. I hope Labor do not under any circumstances get in.

In fact, Abbott is looking by far the more competent and professional of the two majors. By far. Manifest-Destiny or not. Both of the two main parties leave a lot to be desired in terms of visionary policies though. And while the various Mark Latham's of the world may have their flaws [with their giant sized heads the top half of which resemble Volcano-like eruptions of Cranial bone and excessive brain matter or perhaps an Oafish Fist, the sort of physical attribute Einstein and Frankenstein too would have been proud to own].

One of their flaws at least isn't bull.

 Of which labor and the libs have deep reserves of [paul howes']. ie., -A-grade Spin Doctored Bull--it !!

[the Australian Media like to boast how they obliterated this one -Latham- from off of our televisions and other media outlets, as though it's for the good of the Australian people! When really it's because he has ideas and points of views that are not beholden or that kowtow to the 'Mass Media of Murdoch' and the various liberal leftist media [the ABC] and their own God-like opinion of themselves as enforcers of our moral and economic virtue. How peculiar they are.]

My solution, vote either an independent or for Bob Brown and the greens [as much as I disagree with some of their views, particularly on their attitude toward 'Economic' refugees in boat's] with libs as a recourse.

21/8/10-voting day & have decided to go with Abbott. Just seems more competent than labor. esp., when it comes down to boat people and dealing with these effectively. Also a broadband network not as overblown; -Abbott seems little more innovative in his approach, though this maybe typical liberal lack of support for Australian intelligence levels, seeing us as only ever a quarry for the multi-nationals.

Also labor caving in on the resources tax, and only concentrating on Sydney and the hopeless state labor government there, sooo... everything that's wrong with labor -shame Gillard has in the last week finally stopped being less a labor party machine 'functional drone' and shown a side to herself that is quite refreshing. Greens will get my seconds.

21/8/10 1.25pm- went with Labor. As much as think they bunch incompetent chumps. [Libs have simply devolved into too much of a political party for fascists in the last couple of decades for anyone not of the ultra-rich set, to want to vote them in].

Julia Gillard; Party Machine fembot?

Chapter8 AUSTRALIA and the Refugee [2012]

Though undeniably Australia's two main parties are trying to appeal far too much to the redneck lobby and conceivably could allow in more 'real' refugees, not just economic ones who have the money to pay and queue jump. Economic Refugees such as this can come with their own preconceived notions of class, race and nationalistic superiority also, it might be stated.

[This lobby I speak of that I believe is rather inclined toward a more neo-fascist element and is often under the assumed leadership of a certain flame-haired lady who fairly regularly comes and goes just like the attention-seeker she in fact is, and who is not really as in charge as she herself might like to believe. For behind her are the more militant thuggish puppet-masters who will only ever fully display themselves and their true motivations when the need for pretence is no longer there. And where they will undoubtedly assume full control over this woman and this nation, not un-alike the way others have done in other parts of the world in the not too distant past. I refer more directly to Germany's former Weimar Republic converted to fascist state by Hitler and mob].

If per chance this country let in approximately around 80-120,000 or so 'real refugees' every year and for a period of five to ten years, it might not be a bad thing? Maybe also we could cut back on some of the more 'economic refugees' choosing to come here. [Australia's recent generations of young folk have become a little arrogant, self-satisfied and money orientated everything is about big cars, big houses].

Admittedly the associated costs of taking in the dislocated poverty-stricken refugee is another matter because initially their settling in and acclimatizing can subject a country to massive cost over-runs in terms of its social security, special housing needs, educational costs as well as health/medical costs. In fact, it can take a full generation and in some cases far longer before they and their families actually begin to pay their way back to their new homeland as full tax-paying citizens without being fractious in terms of the general economic health of the nation at large.

Ghetto-ism is often regarded as being one of the worst aspects of new immigrants, more especially so if older historical areas succumb to being the enclave of another racial/cultural grouping, making its former inhabitants then start to feel largely excluded or overwhelmed either by sheer numbers or by difference from any further participation in a particular area. Such aspects of 'new arrivals' with novel ways of doing things can be quite scary to have to deal with especially if a particular ethnic enclave has practices within its own community not fully reconciled with the overall wider community. Bringing forth somewhat alienating issues that then become the target of extreme right-wing elements if such issues as ghettoisation does become too persistent.

So in that case these new refugees would probably have to live and take employment in areas other than our major capital cities at least until they have become much more inculcated into the overall community. They might initially be trained and given used in spheres like national service and forestry work or even in major infrastructure projects in parts of the nation most of its inhabitants would prefer not to find themselves, as way of finding their way in their new nation just the way its early pioneer settlers did initially. Nevertheless, if we only put a stop to half of our many New Zealand neighbours who readily take full advantage of Australia in work related areas as well non-work related areas, we could easily bring in an extra 300,000 real refugees alone! Admittedly not all New Zealander's are free-loaders.

Then there are the literally massive amounts of young British, Europeans, Americans backpacker/travellers who naturally assume that they have the right to seek out employment here before heading off with the proceeds to holiday in places like Thailand, and have been doing thus now for well near 40 years or more...without question. Akin to this are huge numbers of Chinese/Indian/other 'students' all being invited into this nation on behalf of the Business & Commerce Councils of Australia in order to seek out work often at the expense of our own youth and even older working populations. All of these sad to say are in the main 'economic refugees' -not real dislocated war-torn or impoverished refugees!

Generally, one could class a political seriously displaced refugee as having no home, no nationality and little real economic circumstances- not just someone who wants to better their circumstances at a particular point in time of economic downturn in their own nation state! And who also might still retain other passports such as a British-euro passport as well as an Australian one while awaiting the right time to then easily depart. Australian born nationals on the other hand are neither desired nor wanted in such climes less they have direct parentage, or unless they are moneyed. It is rarely the other way around unfortunately.

Those Australian born citizens are generally stuck with one passport only, and the restrictions this places upon those born here can at times be much more arduous than it entitles those not born here to practice with relative ease if the wrong economic times should ever prevail! Much of this relates to rather opaque national affirmation issues in terms of constitutional rights and clarification of our true national sovereignty. Are we owned by the Queen of England, the US or are we our own men so to speak?

As to an incoming immigrant's religious practices, let us preference the secular or at least the mildly religious. Certainly not those strongly set mentalities in their particular belief systems whether Christian or Muslim, Hindu or Buddhist. Excessive dogmatism over religion is generally something 'real' refugees do not have either for that matter [meaning excessive god-full-ness, which is often why they have become refugees in the first place?]

There was indeed a time right before the 'John Howard' era in fact when this land was a largely & proudly secular place. Where if one was religious, it was never to be taken entirely seriously. Now you could not say such a thing, because in the last 20 odd years the 'religious' specifically of the Christian variety among us have become as fundamentalist and determined in their attempts to make their particular cult as influential as going to watch the footy or a game of cricket on Saturday as in the good ole US of A.

Our schools are either funded or not much. This depends very much on whether they have at heart a religious core. By being fundamentally Christian in approach or just as intently Jewish or Muslim in conviction. All much enriched by our governments far more so than our secular government high-schools. Secularism or at least religion only on special occasions like at Xmas or possibly when a member of one's family has departed is sadly no longer becoming the Australian mainstream.

For now, days we seem to have become ashamed of our original roots, a time where we found ourselves in this land because we indeed lacked both monetary worth, class respectability or RELIGIOUS DOGMA. It is truly sad to see a nation forced into religious observance of the like of other realms of the globe where the upholding of religion with which to define one's race & culture creates more trouble than its worth?

In fact, is it not high time we started taxing all religion!

It should not be forgotten that Australia has always been far ahead of any other first world country in taking in immigrants and this has been much the case since the 1940's-50's. The great and overarching need however is for this nation to increase the education of its own people and more especially so within the arts & humanities as well massive upskilling in trades education with classifications of the like of engineering/science also being taken into account, because just bringing truck-loads of new citizens with 'cultural values?' into this country can be an adjunct for those who would rid Australia of its redneck ways.

In the end it is only through the implementation of higher standards of education & upskilling that Australian's will become a more focused nation in terms of its industrial /commercial resources and science practices in an innovative manner over which has always been relegated to best practice on the sporting field [which in itself is not bad, as sport can be associated with skill and innovation too], but it is important to keep in mind here that there are very powerful forces much allied toward keeping Australia and Australian's in the land of 'the forever stupefied'-' & 'the basically unskilled.'

Meaning foreign Multi-National entities [principally American interests but also as those of British/European aristocratic ownership and interest who attempt to cheapen democracy in order to bring back Monarchism by stealth], along with the Industrial-Military complex, determinedly concerned with ensuring that Australia's and other non-European realms with their immense mineral/oil resources remain principally under their helmsman ship & control and who are somewhat opposed to us becoming a truly sovereign nation, alas.

2014 the recent death of one of these 'refugee boat people' on Manus island is an indictment on this countries refugee policy which on the one hand allows tens of thousands of so-called economic refugees to flood in under the guise of being either students, travellers or tourists, yet refugees like the man from war-torn Iraq who was cold-bloodedly murdered by a bunch of intolerant, enraged, Papuan racists is allowed [small island nations throughout the pacific region seem to be remarkably adept at this sort of thing actually].

Admittedly they were supposedly coerced into the doing by Australian staff who work on behalf of Serco the company involved in over-seeing this whole mess but undeniably it was ugly race hate that compelled such extremes of murderous rage.

#2015 more recently a man who after being refused citizenship attempted to take his own life, after waiting five long years to hear of his predicament. Now whether he is attempting to emotionally blackmail his way into the country is not the point! The fact that an individual found ill-suited for being a candidate for citizenship had to wait so long for an answer in the first place is more the point. Surely if one's history &/or lack of identification is in the negative their waiting time should be dealt with rather more quickly than five long years in a detention centre however well run or comfortable their detention may appear to be compared to their time spent on a leaky old boat out on the high seas after paying probably vast amounts of money to criminal gangs with which to do so, in their attempts at trying to obtain residency here.

Laborite is as much to blame as Liberal here.

Chapter9 THE AUSTRALIAN MEDIA AS A REPETITIVE IMBECILIC IMPOVERISHED MONSTER

THE AUSTRALIAN MEDIA AS A REPETITIVE IMBECILIC IMPOVERISHED MONSTER

THE AUSTRALIAN MEDIA AS A REPETITIVE IMBECILIC IMPOVERISHED MONSTER

The Australian Media as an impoverished, repetitive, imbecilic, monster [first written in May 2008 but the media are just as bad today probably because there in their final death throes]

Both the commercial and government media in this country are symptomatic of the avaricious, small-minded, mean, self-serving, shallow, ultra-capitalist, white and racist mentality that has pervaded this country throughout most of the 20th-and even now in the early part of the 21st century. You only have to witness the machinations of the local media here to see the emptiness of culture.

One section is riddled with this right-wing, modern, white female-centrism disguised as some virtuous new ideology for humanity when it's basically not. And not only the government equal opportunity regime type media like the ABC but often this same ideology has also inculcated itself much into our commercial media too, while at the same time still being highly prone toward misogynistic, ferociously, over-commercialised tendencies [such as Murdoch's news, Packers channel 9] or else they may contain a mix of this sort of feminist ideological rhetoric in with their commercial protocols for the full advantage [like Stokes' channels 7].

Still however it is really just the 'aussie' media trying to disguise its 'cultural and intellectual shallowness' with this female role-model, feminism as cover for a nation that truly denigrates any sort of high intelligence.

The Australian media however is acutely unaware of how irrelevant and uninvolved it is in actual fact to most reasonably intelligent minded people. And it is the internet thankfully that is catapulting them back to the ground with rather a thud and about time too! They have been getting away with murder and for decades.

Finally with internet blogging many of the people that formerly controlled all the mass media within this country for example its Commercial & Government media including the various newspaper publications of Murdoch, Fairfax-[admittedly The Financial Review is a good newspaper without so much of the silly use of word mantras as part of political correctness], Stokes' West Australian Newspaper [exemplary in its sheer stupidity and ugly tendencies to aim many of its stories at certain individuals that do not go so easily along with the script which in this case is deeply right-wing and Barnett exalting in its orientation. And again a certain unnamed individual is constantly being aimed at by editor after editor, actually most of the small insular Perth media are so-inclined. Now these outlets god-like powers are being finally whittled away, their power of absolute media domination is subsiding. Who watches television anymore?

So no longer are these media outlets the sole virtuous truth.

There are now newer more independent voices to listen to and hear and display and lay open the often insignificant under-intelligence of the formerly unimpeachable job secure dispositions of the journalistic elite and others within traditional media roles, such as -;

Radio National WITH ITS JOURNALISTS THAT TRULY THINK ITS ALL ABOUT THEMSELVES and the values these attempt to instil through their supposed, unbiased reporting,

Perth 'local' radio ABC 720 with people like Geoff Hutchinson that think they're not really shock-jocks and who is often as much caught up in all the politically correct drama and hype, can actually be a very rational and reasonable voice when he tries and stops making it all about themselves! Unalike one JillO who just has her little spiteful artsy agendas particularly against 'one' individual?

And too there are those numerous sporting jocks who on the various commercial outlets like 6PR's as well the Australian Broadcasting Corporation who like to indulge in similar tirades against any hapless individual who they might deem as being up for it because of his/her differing views or even critical opinions as to the sporting media's often [to put it into Australian colloquial terminology] their quite often boof-headed sporting journalist tendencies with which to harangue and try to psychologically torment any member of the community they feel may have slighted them and their politically correct, rhetoric which too often only covers over their right-wing, Anglo-centric agendas and 'ugly' commerciality at all costs.

The worst of these often call Australian Rules Football games and their unrivalled over-use of words like "young" young that young ad-infinitum is utterly pathetic and only makes you want to listen to the calling out of the livestock in a cattle-yard rather than listen to such utter foolishness. 'Talented' another or talent this talent that- how they desperately need to know of a thesaurus in order to see that the English language can really be quite graceful and even poetic and not just mediocre like their on-field sporting heroics. Another word misused or poorly used or just used way too, too much. 'Ugly' as in 'that was an ugly field out there today' 'the ugly pointy-end of the game', there's always ugly in their limited and stupid ugly vernacular. 'Pointy-end' is a new and recent phenomenon addition to their terminology, and again over-used to construct and make their silly, stupid point.

Phillip Adams although a lefty liberal and at least a highly intellectual one is similar as is his colleague at Radio National like one Fran Kelly who is also given to too keenly be a promoter of this sort of clap-trap and over-use of specific and repetitive, word mantra's aimed at a certain individual? Or just any individual who they feel maybe up for a little psychological torment or scrutiny care-of the all-powerful, intimidating force of the rather insular, protected, nepotic Australian media.

Channel sevens Chris Bath is an appalling user of this sort of the word mantra, brain-bombarding approach to the point of being utterly unwatchable, as are her other politically correct ideologue's and/or colleagues especially those on the opposite commercial network Channel Nine with people such as Liz Hayes and her colleagues on that station's Sixty Minutes program especially the rather silly, self-absorbed, personality with obviously good insider networks at the expense of good journalism 'that often absurd, utterly, depressing dullard of a man "Charles Whooley." And unfortunately it is for this sad little fellow 'Woolly by name- Woolly by nature'.

Numerous others with permanent jobs on the ABC television network and Radio national can be very smart but equally depressing because these display a very similar lack of integrity and intelligence and their own penchant for targeting individuals who do not toe the PC line, declaring psychological war on any individual who has the temerity not to fully endorse their particular social manifesto/agenda of the time and who may have question 'the authority of their media' over such things – or any philosophy that would attempt to bely the 'fifth estates' potential for breaking down nepotism and old, out-dated, ideological values and constraints.

This idiot mentality within the Australian mass media that demeans the intelligence of its viewers by taking up certain words or 'mantras' for instance using terminology related to ones intestinal workings with which to describe current economic uncertainty's such as the way Ali Moore did on ABC Lateline business some weeks ago by suggesting to one of her interviewee's as to whether his company had fully 'digested' the full state of the economic climate of late, such silliness is way beneath the journalistic integrity and far too intelligent head of such a woman sadly.

Or the way in which various presenters and newsreaders overuse into the extreme again the adjective 'young' as though repeating such a word over and over gives these some magical hold over their viewer and these will in turn witness higher ratings for their television station or something. And the word friend is another and yes used into oblivion by simplistic out of control undiagnosed fools & nit-wits in the main who have jobs in the media.

Other of these over-used mantras of recent times aimed at the psychological fatigue of those individuals that refuse to be pandered to with all the politically correct ideology are the use of the word 'OPINION' meant to convey that only the media and those individuals that have jobs in such spheres should be allowed to register opinions-disguised as scientific truth.

As well an obsession with words and phrases more lately such as 'oh how sad'- 'just an opinion'- 'ugly this, ugly that' and 'Pick' 'picking' and the word YOUNG that belies any journalistic intellectual level or the credibility of even our most respected journalists/ intellectual elites.

Listen to ABC classical music radio for examples of those with high-brow ideas but seriously dull-brow, parroting of ideological political correctness and you could be forgiven for being under the impression that such music truly was meant for intelligent people. The more high-brow, affected and somewhat activist female presenters on ABC Classic radio are especially prone to such mannerism's, hell-bent on ensuring they put stress upon certain words like 'OPINION'-'YOUNG'-'TALENTED'-'BRAVE' and 'HEROIC' with lemming-like obligation to do as they have been advised ? By the fashion more like it.

Maybe it's all kind of a water torture instrument meant for certain individuals that resent being brainwashed by greedy, self-serving, manipulative over-paid, power-obsessed idiots or do not appreciate being regarded as sacrificial lambs for the use of religion [which would explain why one presenter is especially prone to such mannerisms ie., Geraldine Doogue who is often prone to this little psychological harassment campaign aimed at an unnamed individual for his lack of promotion of her particular religious sympathy's and his unwillingness not to be part of their little agenda in which his role is to play the modern messiah, then die and let the whole vile nonsense carry-on for another millennia or two?].

Besides this most of the media personalities that constantly over-emphasise expressions like 'YOUNG' or 'YOUTH' or 'TALENTED' or 'HEROES' are rarely if ever young or of youth themselves with many of them above or over, well over in fact the age of 25 with at best an average intelligence and a mediocre arrogance related to their own particular talents. Often as not they are well into their mid to late thirties 40's 50's 60's and have rarely moved aside for anyone other than their own mirror image, and have certainly never made way for those considered more talented, heroic, intelligent, younger, prettier or handsomer than themselves.

So as well being your typical fuckwit these could easily be referred to as hypocrites also.

Such ridiculous extremes of imbecility basically because our media is full off its own self-importance and has been so long now in the hands of hangers-on and cretins or other such left-over spivs and much alike our big banks and telecommunications areas [Telecom] have just never had to lift their act which is true for much of the Australian Arts and Literary establishments and elitist intellectual community in general actually.

They've been so over-regulated and protected they've become smug and by degrees inane and quite incestuous.

The Government needs to just de-regulate this countries media the way they've done everything else [except big banks and large foreign multi-nationals]. Not with foreign news media we are already much dominated by these, and anyway networks like the BBC is another example of this kind of mentality also highly prone to this sort of specific word association and repetitiveness sadly.

Preferably we need more really independent news networks from within not without, as well our televisual media should be more truly representational of Australia's real ethnic mix and not be mostly made up of one particular racial stereotype/grouping who tend to be of somewhat nepotistic/insider backgrounds mostly, [blithely unaware of how these do not represent the complete mix of Australia's over-all racial identity].

Deregulation is needed within the mass media of this nation, [even with all the internet bloggers] because it is so obvious these are incapable of conducting themselves in neutral non-biased ways and that too often use their chosen field of profession as a form of power seeking tool with which to target individuals who do not weakly accept their rule.

In fact, complete and utter deregulation should be the real magical word 'Mantra' when it comes to the Australian media.

26/3/13- in recent times the 4-5 big boys who control 95% of this countries media [Stokes, Packer, Fairfax, Murdoch] have all used their newspapers, radio and television stations and other types of media influence in order to make their most important news story all about 'how the governments new media laws are going to make this countries media less diverse'.

That's diversity speaking for ya right there!

14/9/2014;- My, my! How the media have somersaulted anew? There have been in the last few years phenomenal changes since this piece was first written and with the internet being these days most people's main resource for obtaining either their news, current affairs and other type of education and cultural enlightenment or just different opinions we now witness new and positive change which has brought about far less arrogance on the part of old media and much more intelligence to new and contemporary journalism as well as new personalities who even without the right insider contacts possibly because of a well-read blog instead of insider contacts are often invited onto the big media to expound on some topic in general. It's been quite amazing the change in the last few years alone.

-Oh! doubtlessly there are still lots of idiots out there particularly within the sporting media and hopefully with time all these morons will die out and sport will become far less revered or at least called out by far more articulate people-hopefully!

And I still have my car discretely entered into by elements who may have been put up to it by those with mostly hostile intentions who then go onto expound in round about ways for the ears of all those in the 'know' who are maybe rather hostile toward me and my unwanted 'opinions'. Such as articles of clothing or writings disseminated against my wishes by those with access to my computer or otherwise by stealing the contents of my notebooks etc, etc. Which are then usually surreptitiously made fun off, or used to cite an example of some cause the media maybe given to at a specific period of time?

Something that has been going on now for a very long time actually ie., scrutinization and psychological harassment directed toward myself by our media because of whom I am and whatever I may have been known for. All as a form of payback for daring to challenge them, or either from not toeing 'their' line by being a good little sacrificial victim to the great 'god of the media' and possibly through such means help to propagate a new religious experience in a kind of messianic way for the dawning of this the new 'era.'

But either way we have now vast new areas of experience and diversity c/o the Internet that has somewhat transcended the domination of old Media. It has been a long time coming but can only get better.

Chapter10 POPE FRANCIS and THE VATICAN
[Protestantism/Anglicans and the 'American Evangelists' both black and white included]

Portrait of the myth, the man the dogma? [2008]

The obsession these old men of the Vatican like Pope Francis have with the crucified figure of an overtly muscular, very healthy, white Anglo-Saxon male, naked and bloody on a cross speaks volumes for a Church and a Religion that at its heart is disturbing and ultimately very negative. A beautiful image it maybe, but it is also hideous at the same time. An image that appeals to two of the worst aspects of the human psyche, both narcissism & cruelty in order to assuage some ancient, appeasement based on guilt to the gods that rule over us from heaven above. Thereby sacrificing someone, or something as way of investing the sacrificed with some kind of fake sense of redemption and spirituality by being sacrificed.

After-all the whole Jesus thing is little more than the Prometheus myth retold. And even before the Greek god Prometheus there was the Egyptian God Phoenix, with similar mythology. It's obvious the early Jesus cultists were well researched and pretty enterprising too for that matter. And who gets to play this sacrificed Jesus for these ancient conniving Pharaohs who down through the ages have quietly changed and manipulated the people over and over again using such a sacrificial character one has to ask? Our Pharaohs never sacrifice though do they?

No doubt some poor bastard who's either been unwittingly, ceremoniously slung into an anachronistic cauldron run by spiritual fakes, or more likely some poor unbeknown sod who has rather been shanghaied against his/her own free-will into playing the modern returned 'Jesus figure' for the 20th and 21st centuries...because if such a person had have been asked up front no doubt there would have been a case of outright refusal to obey the instigators of all of this self-serving nonsense and great and higher purposes/commands.

It can surely be guaranteed that the sort of righteous folk who like this kind of thing are on an intellectual level very shallow people indeed. Mindlessly shallow as well as being rather pretentious in appearing to be without even a shadow of the materialist?

The same sort of people who think so many of these supposed iconic celebrity's & rocks stars are really very, deep, meaningful, souls and not just preppy, nepotistic sociopath's who often as not come these days with two and three generations of familial or insider career networks that make their not inconsiderable talents largely worthless without the attachment of their much more talented forbearers names behind their curriculum vitas.

The 'one' little thing they all have in common is the desire for a resurgent Christian ideal, as in a white mythological returned Jesus figure to be denoted as 'the one.' Their Jesus will be white and plainly suited to the securing of their own racial and hereditary status long into the future. Most behind this whole conspiracy and it is a conspiracy, are essentially upper-middle class white racists including many of the black people who dare to go along with this agenda.

Again the type of folk inured to this sort of thing are usually from pretty, upper-middle class backgrounds which explains the rosy-eyed world view and somewhat idealistic nature they tend towards others esp., those from lower socio-economic backgrounds. They're most definitely not from low or working class backgrounds that can be guaranteed! And rarely is the sacrificial victim a nice, well educated, upper-middle class rich kid, it would have to of course be generally and stereotypically someone of low economic means with little familial backup who is seen to be and considered disposable enough to suit the evil minds behind such religious/spiritual machinations engineered to facilitate and expunge some unconscious corrupt guilt the wider body politic senses of itself.

 If these church/religious leaders [pharaohs] like the new media savvy and 'enlightened' newly elected Pope Francis and his kind ever had their 'Jesus' actually arrive back on earth one day in order to seek his ownership of 'their' control and stewardship of the Christian church's [both the catholic and protestant churches, and all of these little

Jesus based churches & cult's about] with all of its accoutrement and lucre guarded jealously by these Holy-Men and women, Priests, Popes, Bishops included, all for his own personal usage, quite possibly to use for acquiring land in the best parts of the world with which to fashion a majestic home or two upon in which he might also choose to partake of various high-class whores, an assortment of vestal virgins and other fleshly pursuits- maybe like a nice collection of art and trinkets, perhaps even some nice and expensive wines / spirits/ cocaine, maybe a little yacht or three-none of which happened to be under 60 foot in length and perhaps a little gambol here n there at various casino,...

-I feel damnably sure that the slitherer's who now watch over the various Christian church would very quickly have their 'lord Jesus' quietly hung, drawn and re-crucified before the deadly hour of dawn preferably before the sun was set.

All to ensure that all the excessive power, glitter, gold and other largesse like the vast holdings of real estate that these churches/religions own was never lost from their controlling, greedy, insidious, tenacious and grasping hands basically.

Jesus if he did exist was after all only an intellectual who one surely doubts would have welcomed his thoughts and actions being taken up as dogma and the made into mental slavery all for the sake of religion. He must be rolling in his long lost grave. The real truth of the matter may well be that this 'historical figure' of which there is nil factual evidence of his actual existence in reality, because when one examines the climate of that time it is highly likely that those behind such a figure or messiah were in fact the Romans themselves who took the opportunity of the Jewish cult of waiting for a returned messiah or Christ, by transplanting their own messiah one suited much to their

purposes of undermining Jewish rebelliousness often violent and highly anti-pathetic toward the Roman occupation of Palestine. This new messiah Jesus would propose pacifism and turning of the cheek as the new philosophy, even when one was being stoned, burned or other even more dastardly forms of abuse stemming from any criticism of Rome and its policy toward dissent.

Chapter11 "Howards End" [2005]

-revised article on the electioneering of both the liberal and labor parties of a new election year.

Incorporating thoughts on potential infrastructure reform and for the possibility of an Australian style constitutional Republic.

Along the lines of 'Not' being one is the real damaging thing to us both economically and in terms of our statehood.

While admittedly only ever having voted for the liberals once [Hewson in 93 even when I actually liked Keating, it's just he was surrounded by so many corrupt, weaklings] so bias is not my strong point here, what a relief it will be to see the end of the Howard/Costello regime. And this new Rudd initiative promising broadband should be the final nail to this liberal coffin.

Such an unrelentingly backward looking, conservative even dull government have they been, as well so intent on ensuring this country is forever under the preserve of either foreign multi-nationals-mining baron's or other assortment of rich [mainly via overseas shareholders who in the main are British and strongly connected to the English landed aristocracy].

Forget about anything truly progressive or forward looking from these men and women of the Anglo-sphere. Forget progression into alternative areas of thought such new technologies like the potential from wind, wave, solar or other green related technologies. No we get 'sol' [Solomon Lew] without the solar. Promoting the great cause of 'nuke' technology, without the clear or the green.

12 years is far too long to be without a genuine alternative opposition.

Interesting to now witness the fear and trepidation upon Liberal Party eyes so caught out from behind the glare of finally having some political competition, for the hearts & minds of the Australian populace. They are looking distinctly like an assortment of petrified rabbits. Desperately striving to come up with anything of political value or interest in order to remain relevant until the next election. With the likes of Downer going 'ga, ga' about how Labor should let their man Santoro of the hook now he's lost his place in government. It's all about humanitarianism, -"leave the man be' pleads Downer in heart-rending fashion. Truly!

We witnessed the man himself Howard just like little house-mouse sliding down an airplane shaft very nearly expunged by all the surrounding smoke [and mirrors] and accompanied by our servicemen play acting to a television crew. Expect him next to make a speech sometime in the near future declaring an Al-Qaeda terrorist under the bed of every man and good woman of Australia.

With Costello blaring out like a caterwaul about the sheer lunacy of the broadband initiative and how it's likely to be really, really good for Australia, but really, really bad for him and his wasp mates in and round the Toorak cappuccino strip as well being something his bunch are just too backward looking to see the use of because quite possibly it will result in Australia becoming more and more independent and progressive as a nation and not so easily beholden to just the big mining companies and other major foreign multi-national corporates.

Then we've got jug-head Brendon [onward Christian soldiers subtly intimidating any critic of the Howard regime with extermination or eternal damnation if they so much as dare to criticise Howard with 'one' critic in particular being singled out! Gee I wonder who that might be?] Nelson and all his devotion to purchasing American made armaments -usually 30 years out of date. But heh! Brendon knows the yanks love him for it and might even make him a national hero like they've done to the Prime Minister whom they've canonised into American political celebrity. Brendon Nelson who likes to screech down at us through the television set at how the western world is going to cave-in, if we don't re-elect John Howard at the next election!!

So we have old copper technology going up against new fibre broadband technology. So far, so good. Let's have an election and a new modernist socially broadened Government, that is government for all, not the minority like we've had with the previous two and this is something Rudd needs to be wary of. Nevertheless, 'it's time'.

Of course the opposition leader has to do more than be seen to be wearing hard hats whilst shovelling coal or fabricating his personal history in order to appeal to the average Australian voter. As well as initiating his new broadband plan the labor party should attempt to alleviate this malaise of guilt, fear, dread and self-loathing Australians have been putting themselves through over the last three decades [brought on by the signing of Gatt Agreements of 74 by Fraser/liberals] by effecting and bringing forth vast and dynamic infrastructure projects that involve not just communications but also engineering projects that amount to bringing water from Australia's northern parts via pipelines and specifically down through central western Australia towards Kalgoorlie in order to be pumped back downwards to Perth, rather than to just continuously keep trying to use up ever more of the water reserves of the Yarrigadee basin.

This would result in opening up much of this nation's interior resulting in real benefits for our indigenous and many other isolated towns that may well take pressure off this countrie's overuse of its coastal resources. There would be massive outcomes and benefits if projects such as this were realised in so many ways.

All the fears from the feminists and environmentalists etc., are somewhat overwrought and ultimately to this nations detriment in that their only ever viewing or valuing our great northern region in purely touristic/wildlife terminology is somewhat self-interested, indeed quite wrong for many others, especially those of the indigenous community.

We have been compelled by the travails and sacrifices of these individuals [the environmentalists] to take seriously the natural aspect of our continent and rightfully so, but neither should we begin to overvalue it to the point of never harnessing its potential for the betterment of the human condition. So as well as value the more spectacular and sacred parts of it we should be reminded too that much of it is not wilderness but could actually be seen as unrelenting, wasteland where not mankind but only flies and never ending saltbush and dust coat its surface.

Probably one of the best things Australia could do for critics of environmental vandalism would be to try to develop a much vaster rail capacity especially for urban/city dwellers in order to lessen their need to use the vehicle something this country has been sadly lacklustre in bringing about. As well dare it be said a reduction in the overall size of our urban city sprawl. A new generation of denser, urban communities, interwoven with more natural reserves as well a closer relationship with local agriculture?

A TVG train-line from Perth to the east coast would also resolve the dread of distance traveller's face by land from one side of the continent to the other. The French have just obliterated the land speed record and done it using rail some 570km per hour. You would have to doubt that the cost of doing such a thing here would not pay for itself in anytime at all. That trip is an unrelenting singularly overlong bum-wrecking boar of a trip that unless one gets absolutely sloshed on the way over, it is very easy to never, ever want to undertake the experience again, for many at least. But going close to 600km an hour would bring a thirty-hour journey down into a heart pumping 12-16hr trip of a lifetime.

As well a train-line connecting West from the Kalgoorlie region into Alice Springs and onwards into the northern parts of Queensland is long overdue.

You have to ask why do things like this rarely if ever get done in this relatively young open pristine generously advantaged and opportunity blessed nation of ours at least it was like that at the turn of the century. Somewhere somehow something else has taken over. A malaise-like guilt about being an Australian.

Rudd must bring about a new tariff reform and a new constitutional mandate for Australia [incorporating a contemporary idea of an Australian republic into the 21st century, and hopefully a new flag] and give back to native born Australians a country to proudly call their own like every other nation on earth has the right to do and is not in any danger of giving up. Even though these [particularly the Europeans, Japanese, north Americans] continuously keep countries like Australia optimistic that one day they will fully open up and remove their own trade barriers one must doubt the seriousness of their intentions. There simply is too much to lose. And is this not the real reason behind why this country has lost its capacity for scope and vision [a kind of totalitarian feminisation of Australia meant to 'feel good' and civilized, but has it failed and resulted in other negatives?]. Risk is not the kind of outcome shareholders want esp., overseas ones and so therefore Australian industry potential must submit to unimaginative and unchallenging ideas of what the potential of this nation could possibly be if truly responsible for its own destiny.

It seems absurd to be paying high prices for produce imported thousands of miles away when local farmers and the like cannot get their produce onto Australian supermarket shelves. And so much of this produce comes in rotten or overpriced without a full acknowledgment of its source or its environmental health viability. To many people's mind that are looking for an alternative to the Howard / Liberal government it could be noted that if Rudd does not offer some better alternatives other than same old same old ie., another power engorged government of an opposing spectrum but with the same style of easy jobs for the boys [and girls] he must not be persuaded into thinking the Australian voter will give him a go only for the sake of it.

It's now time for a state of renewal and a rethink of the scale of Australia not just in terms of vast spaces but also in ways of mind and the imagination, and this will no doubt upset many of a type that fit the wowser and fear of heights category. Rudds promise of broadband is a great start but one would hope this is not the limit to his bravery.

Chapter12 Beauty [2007]

This morning at the department of social security my eyes set upon the type of girl that makes your jaw hit the floor and then proceeds to make your tongue slowly tumble out of your mouth like red carpet being rolled out at some glamorous Hollywood celebrity do. She was with a rather average 'aussie' guy and although Caucasian in appearance the look of his skin tones suggested he may have been of mixed heritage one possibly owing some distant connection to either a Mediterranean or even North African ancestry. Dressed in black t-shirt, daggy jeans & thongs and who would have been round his early to mid-twenties having the kind of hang-dog expression about his face that said 'entirely grateful but also a little overwhelmed please somebody help me out here'.

His girl was at least 3-4 inches maybe 5" inches taller than he and must have been round the 6ft 2-3" mark and then only in a pair of flat scuffs. She was as black as the night and had the most perfectly formed features in both her face and body. Any one scrutinizing her face would surely behold the owner of a pretty up-turned & rather delicate little nose, where just below were bold, beautiful, and quite fulsome lips that framed her not large mouth, all the while owning the kindest, sweetest, almondesque's for eyes I've ever encountered.

Her head was mounted upon a neck as long and graceful as that of a swans with hair closely cropped and featherlike in its curlicue Negroid neatness, typical for some races of Africa esp., those of the Nubian and Ethiopian races, topped with a trucker cap its shade piece 3 quarter turned towards the back as is the fashion, her breasts were well-shaped & womanly, and her legs descended literally forever from her fine smallish but well turned up behind, ever on downwards to where her long narrow feet co-existed with the floor.

It was hard to take your eyes off of her as she with her long arms hung them over the shoulders of her poor 'sub-standard' bogan boyfriend and at other times massaged his shoulders as they both sat and gazed up at the television screen and awaited their appointment with an attendant.

As well as wearing a cap in reverse style she wore purple tights underneath a bleached tiny Denim skirt, the top part of her shapely torso was partially covered by a black T-shirt open sleeved and loose in the true bogan style familiar with the Australian working classes. Sun-Glass's sat atop her cap, her ears held deep drop earrings, with little to no make-up.

And with seemingly no desire to make a big deal out of her obvious physical delights, she came across entirely at ease with being probably the most beautiful girl ever without in the slightest way seeing her all too abundant beauty as though it were an Asset. -Like the way many females are given to do, who have 'some' beauty, but own way more hard-nosed cynicism along with it. And who then go on to commercialize it, live glamorous highly paid Goddess-like lifestyles in the realms of either cinema, television or other modes of celebrity. It's not an unsaid thing to express but it's a definite truism that the most beautiful things quite like the dazzling stars above are seen at their best when they are shaded amidst only the deepest darkest of nights.

Chapter13 Aboriginal Massacres?

This nation was not settled by shiny, happy people. [2012]

It was settled through massacre. The frontier wars here were as murderous and savage as they were in the United

States/Canada or New Zealand. This nation in fact was largely founded on institutionalised racism with a keen sense and even a fondness for cruelty. Which has been its one great mainstay, in that many of its immigrants were those who it could possibly be described as somewhat intolerant of others. Whether they came here from the British Isles, Europe or even Asia. Basically we do like our immigrants to have strong un-altering dispositions...and especially of recent times money, much of it if at all possible.

Commonly expressed these days by the very culture of the place, its obsession with sport, its anti-art, anti-intellectual tendencies, its overall aggression, its obsession with the Nanny-State and particularly with regard to its treatment of asylum seekers and the dispossessed both home and away. A soft, semi-fascist snarling, mean-hearted dog is in reality this nations true and closest friend...alas.

Our first settlers were bloodied, dirty, diseased, poorly educated and often desperate when they arrived throughout the early parts of the 1800's. Throughout much of the 18 century on up until the early twentieth century the greedier & plunderous of them i.e., the rich, bullying landed gentry along with the aid of their bully-boys took such activity into out-right massacre. And such massacres were not few, they were numerous and nasty and were not unaided by biological warfare and the more ignorant working class settler from Britain who were intent on moving into and working the land this rich landed gentry employed them on and empowered them to do.

Disease killed and cleared the new land of many of these indigenous no doubt, as did happy integration but so did plunder and intimidation. And massacre. By a people whom to us today would be somewhat foreign and not easily sympathised with. They were largely British born and British in their identity principally of Scotch-Irish descent ['Ulstermen' who were mainly called upon and used thus because of their propensity for ignorance, violence and an immovable love of 'gods law' above all other laws, by English Royalty since the middle-ages. Where ever these English monarchs wanted to reign. Our early European settlers came with decidedly, ignorant and foreign points of view not inured or well-read as regards their new lands nature and scope.

Nevertheless, the murder and massacre were numerous and perpetrated on both sides though much more done against the indigenous than done to. Particularly when a pastoralist's cattle may have been slaughtered or taken without due concern.

[although in all truth when one adds up the final inter-racial toll one would easily suggest that the damage done is as much in favour of aboriginals than those regarded as 'non-indigenous,' especially when one considers the modern era and all the rapes committed, then the outright vandalism or murder based upon race].

For all that bad early history however which can never be retracted unless one comes up with a time machine of sorts and even then? Probably not. What can be done however is recognition of the fact that this nation's first beginnings were brutal and unequal and dispossession was to the advantage of the white European settler not the local indigene. Like it or not. To deny this is akin to driving blindly down the streets with no brakes and blithely hoping that everything is going to be okay. This kind of ignorance will ensure that Australian culture will remain forever in a kind of, 'she'll be right' denial mentality...just don't mention it and it will all go away.

Sometimes just mention it and it will still stay there but what goes is the ignorance. What comes about though is the culture.   Meaning Europe and the rest of the world has a history littered with the murdered, the extinct, the dispossessed. In fact, most of this nations immigrants have their own history of dispossession be it from the time of the Romans or further back, where the various Picts who largely lived and roamed in hunter gatherer fashion throughout western Europe as well many other tribes of pre-Roman Europe would probably have the right to demand retrieval of culture & lands if present inheritors could possibly prove that they were of that ilk originally.

As would many ethnicities' who came after and somehow got incorporated into the vastness of European culture. Asia would be as similar, probably thousands of different tribes and ethnicity's got made into some collection of people or civilization there somewhere along histories winding road. Its childish and just plain absurd to think that the whole world will do an abrupt time reversal just to amend one's particular grievances as many of our 'aboriginals'-'indigenous'-'first-peoples,' -'hunter gathers' seem to want to do. Life unfortunately goes on.

The history must not be ignored however. That's the significant thing. The leftist extreme do not agree on that though, they want to somehow over-turn the facts and make everything go back to the way it was. Good luck to them if they know something everybody else does not! My solution to curb some of the blissful, ignorance and refusal to think of such things as massacres happening -is to create a monument to such tragic history especially history appropriate to Western Australia, a state especially prone to the culture of denial, as though if people suddenly accept such historical fact we are all going to disappear down a funnel into the bowels of the earth.

-[especially by those in 'Real Estate Developers Land' hungrily suburbanising & cementing over so much of our beautiful South-West region this very moment and who greatly need to recognize this land is essentially stolen land, -although maybe that's the real problem in truth?]

This idea is to make a great monument just like we do for the boys who fought in various war-zones and other conflicts and that sit in many of our cities/towns throughout the country. Only instead of a monument to war and sacrifice, this will be a monument to our original Anglo-centric, Christian ignorance, and will be in recognition of this sacred cow of unstated denial. Something which is as much a part of the new Australian migrant mindset whether they have just come here from either Asia/Britain/Europe or elsewhere and who often come with highly ignorant and even quite racist appraisals of aboriginal Australia.

I'd like to make a monument to Yagan but different to the one executed previously by a local Perth sculptor from the 1970's a certain Robert Hitchcock and which now sits on a lonely non-descript piece of island bushland where no one has to see it and bear witness to this somewhat shameful past grievance.

A Yagan it must be said which is rather poorly rendered and which bears only a passing resemblance to true Yagan except for the fact Yagan was tall, had a beard and also carried a spear.

I mean no disrespect to the sculptor but to be honest his Yagan looks 'like a virgin'. And his depiction of the human form is sadly lacking in both realism, realization, imagination, vision and depth of meaning. It looks much like a generic form of some comic book cut-out of your typical superhero figure, or maybe a manikin of the ideal male body which is then used as a display in a clothes shop outlet. Basically it's not good.

I want to sculpt a real magnificent Yagan. One that is aboriginal of that time in physique and attitude. Noble but also brutal. Savage but wiry. Athletic with scar tissue, but also having lean muscle fibre along with those slender, thin ankles common for aboriginal Australia. A fierce indomitable tribal expression to go with. A less than noble beast but still classic and a figure to be respected. And one not laughed at or so easily dismissed as puerile that gets vandalised on lonely nights by having its head removed.

Because the great figure I will sculpt will not only be superbly realized [by my formidable capacities to sculpt the human figure like few others, certainly in this land and further still] -my Yagan will not have to be vandalised. In that he will not have a head to be vandalised with...

His head removed by the colonial force at the time will be in his own hand, bloody and dripping, and thrust forth to us his executioners in denial- we the viewer who might happen to be one of an audience looking up to Yagan beside the beach and who may be given to thought about ideas such as class, race, subjugation by the rich of yesterday and indeed today who often are the same people.

His giants head held out in one hand and presented as a gift to the viewer below with his own hand will have the fierce, Neanderthal but still pensive browed, broad nosed, look about it. A slightly open-mouthed expression either from shock or despair. Thick locks of hair not unlike some primordial angry, cave-dwelling genius from a darker-age, the age before 1770. His long legs and figure will not have the idealism and heroic pose of modern steroidal masculinity that we know of in the present time.

Instead he will have the difficult awkwardness of figure not unalike Rodin's great figures particularly the stance of his walking man series [St. John figures].

And to his Yagan's rear, as if shorn from off his shoulder blades and set upon a high post at an angle in degree say about 45 degrees, will be the vast outstretched wings of the Wedge-Tailed eagle surrounding him at least more to one side than the other, but still distinctly protective/and releasing. An assignation endorsing him to be the leader of his tribe.

While his spear will be thrust into the ground beside him one hand holding it but not angrily, just with a sort of concentrated intensity, as if clarifying his malcontent and defiance over his loss of homelands.

I choose to call this statue, "Black Angel; A Monument to Yagan." I would set this sculptural monument at one of Perth's major city beaches, such as 'City Beach' in the Floreat, Shenton Park precinct, because of its salubrious somewhat consumer-nicety, its slightly conservative outlook, certainly because of its centrality and potential for open public space [that is if I can get the local council to allow such a thing of which they can be rather immune to simply because Perth is such a racist city in a racist state]. Then of course there are my very discreet, bourgeoisie, art-snob, vipers throughout the Western Australian 'jewish' dominated, funded and owned arts community.

Not that their all like that because probably the best art teacher I ever knew was actually its print-making teacher who was undoubtedly a Zionist in his makeup even to the point of disabusing the aboriginals, but he was also an especially great art teacher it must be said [at least before I got harassed via art-politics out of Claremont art school in my teen years and numerous times since-as is not uncommon for those of certain dispositions who the establishment doesn't want to go further in the field of art practice, purely because this might amount to competition. Actually a major problem with any person attempting to establish themselves as a visual artist in this Country-Nepotism 'big time']. And from character assassination via book or song or even via mural these are usually the ones who generally win at end of day.

And no doubt these saboteurs, who most likely have already viewed this post, are right this very minute coming up with a simulacra based upon this very idea, [a few changes here n' there maybe], as well making it clear how this idea of theirs had been thought up a year or two in advance of my own] in order to trump my proposal and make their own submission the more accepted one. With the aid and favour of all their politically correct mates in the arts funding establishments like the Australia Council and elsewhere?

Nevertheless, my bronze Yagan will not be a syrupy, white man's wet dream all about doing the right thing by the aboriginals and coming up with something largely insipid and watered down. It will be much too magnificent for mere pretence. It will no doubt be hated by certain reactionaries in fact much of Perth one should think, but then again I will not be doing it for nil.

As to my price for such a monument it will be right because this sculptural monument will be of quality. And with time 20-30 years such a monument should become if not loved certainly valued and respected if not because of its brilliance as a piece of formal public sculpture, then maybe one would hope for its familiarity.

And it will awaken true history but not make Australians have to feel more guilt at least in the long term. But it will make them more cultured but with more than just eye candy or through creating some weird form of the sort of thing which has become all pervasive in western art these days and especially Australian western art which basically has become too scared to say something deep and meaningful or otherwise all the government bureaucrat's will become quite upset. Such a thing should impart real depth of culture for all Australians whether they agree with Yagan and the aboriginal cause or not. It doesn't really have to matter.

The cost upwards of three million. My cut 2-3m. The cost of materials 1-2millions especially related to foundry work which I will have done here if possible, or France. Where they have a history of doing the very best bronze foundry work. But since I have not had a lot of experience building public monuments the cost may well be higher or lower. If so my price will depend on such outcomes.

Nevertheless, this sculpture of Yagan will be 8-10 feet tall, not including granite lined plinth 6 feet long, 4 feet wide 4 feet high, set upon steps of three -each 2 ft deep. The whole thing should be 15-25 ft tall approx.

It will also thrust me to the very top of the Australian sculptors/art ranking's as not only the highest paid artist in this country [which should not be regarded as entirely self-serving because this might also aid my fellow artists to seek out and even receive better payment rates for their own work by making artists similar in their professional regard not unlike a leading executives would be regarded by the business community-so any monetary value I get from such a proposal means little and I would do it freely if I thought this would give me more than just prove of my abilities.

The money alas will let those in the art world know for once and for all that all their dirty acts of sabotage and exclusion, all their little allegiances and spiteful character assassination behind my back is to nought because I am now the highest paid artist if not in the world certainly within this country and certainly one of its greatest geniuses-not them and their stupid small-minded niggling highly connected friends.

That's what the evil monetary reward will do for me unfortunately, as well get me one or two other things one of which will be to possibly depart this nation and find some place where people do not despise those with initiative and an ounce of talent that is not only of the sporting variety, but without doubt what this proposal should do to my reputation is to make me probably as regarded and respected as any other contemporary Australian artist within this country.

Even above all my fellows whom are generally female, aboriginal, ethnic or if of male gender these are usually white, Jewish, homo-sexual and definitely from a bourgeoisie well-connected background. I shall be the first who is male from a genuinely non-privileged, working class orientation. One will simply not be able to write about this nation's art history without including my work from here on.

So two birds will be gotten by one significant stone- I shall become both the highest paid artist as well the most exemplary and important Australian artist of my or any other generation!

And the most important thing such a sculpture might do, what it will in fact do! is to make this nation more levelled and less inclined toward reactive violence in its nature, it would not so need to be the nanny-state it has become, it would lose this need to drive huge familial trucks [Suv's] throughout our streets and call them cars, it would be less paranoid about children and young adults, it would become less dumb, and much less essentially so upper-middle class feminist-riven as well our arts & culture would be less dominated by an insular, class-bigoted left holier than thou mentality that may not believe in god but they surely do see themselves as god sometimes!!

Eyes now so 'Wide shut' would become 'Eyes Wide awake'.

Chapter14 Same Sex Marriage Equality [2011]

Finally, homosexuals have their human rights [same-sex marriage] recognized by our new Labor Govt. This is not a bad thing? Now maybe you will be able to go to a public toilet and not have to put up with suppressed freaks looking for a touch-up or an anal intercommunication experience. -Or have to put up with these same sort of people living the lie trying to act all moustachioed, red-blooded and hetero by marrying a female partner all the while continuing to entertain sex with other men behind their spouse's back.

The sooner they are allowed to be open and honest about their sexuality the better. I just wish all the religious right-wingers would realize this. But that's the problem with those reactionaries within conservative politics [and religion] unfortunately. Many of them are suppressing their innate homo-sexuality! -Hence the need to inflict hate & prejudice campaigns all in the name of Jesus and good & wholesome Christian values.

We might also begin to see less War and class politics, or is that expecting too much? If only they [the conservatives] would get to the crux of the matter. And that is unfortunately that they are a hive of repressed gayness. But am so happy Labor has done this finally. Repression is never a good thing. Sooner it is done with the better.

Possibly too the arts and higher learning faculty's within this country will finally accept heterosexual males and not chastise or be so prejudiced against them as way of effectively dumbing them down in order to keep Gays' on top of the social/intellectual hierarchical ladder?

#24th/5/2015 Ireland has seen fit to allow gay marriage, 52% for. One never expected this in religious very conservative Ireland!! Change is good. And really if one looks at the way straights carry-on about the importance of a man and woman as primary parents to children this is bunk. The amount of abuse and bad rearing that goes on in straight parent relationships only confirms this!

I'm sure there will be homosexual marriages that are disastrous too when it comes to the raising of children but will they be any worse than what we've had over the last two thousand years with man & woman only marriage partners.

There will be good and bad of it no doubt but in the end this will clear up a lot of rot that now goes on and has been going on for a long time especially in straight society and what they are seen to be. If I do have a concern over homosexual marriage it is that this may entitle them even more privilege and power over and above the non-homosexual community because of their generally clubby and protective connections and network mentality used against straights competing in similar areas of life and usually being excluded by the gay-militia from doing so.

This could result in even more serious socio/economic inequality issues falling into the hands of the homosexual community at the detriment of the heterosexual community and where they must comply to this other sex even more so than they do now in important areas of our life. Not at a street level admittedly although that could be argued against too if one really wanted but more so in higher learning areas of life and work. There are whole areas of this that are held as sacred to essentially the homosexual gender like the arts and this nonsense that only 1% of the population are gay is a nonsense. I think a significant aspect of our general population are in fact homosexually inclined i.e., more like 15-25%? Which means they have not only great economic wealth but they also have and always have had great political/social cache-power. Let us not delude ourselves about this issue!

Essentially, marriage equality is a good thing but we do need caution, because let us not fool ourselves that the passive-aggressive tendencies associated with many of these special interest groups particularly within the LGBT communities could easily qualify such groups as being orientated towards having authoritarian tendencies if and when they ever got total control over the majority and with such passive-aggressive natures a totalitarian 1984 could well eventuate, in that these would be happy to shut down free-speech over little more than hurt feelings.

Chapter15 If Woman Ruled the World? [92]

even more thoughtless thoughts ; if females ruled the world

-[after an essay first written 92 since revised & re-written 2010]

Really one of the main reasons why this country comes over as so fundamentally patriarchal is because we are not a very creative or for that matter very intelligent culture [Sport rules as does the Resource industry and other primary commodity industries]. And this exacerbates the situation of Australia's supposed patriarchal culture the way hot water does on sunburn.

I do not honestly know how giving women all these high income jobs is essentially going to change things much except more low income aussie males are going to become more ignorant and sports loving and Neanderthal like.

I'd like to state here how I feel much of Feminism is a con and is essentially constructed by certain high income alpha males with a view to enticing females into their fold, as well keep other competing males in quite lowly positions economically i.e., a vast supply of low income-low skilled workers, as well a large supply of men for the military. -Of which females never get to do the dirty hard bloody stuff do they? Such as slice off half the face of a young 16 yr old recently conscripted soldier or perhaps rape and disfigure a young virgin then slice her throat in order to avoid the consequences of military justice, or possibly slaughter a helpless old woman desperately cowering and attempting to cover over the weak frailty of her husband and then watch the blood drip from her throat before spearing him through the neck. Or even come back from service with appalling injuries from being on the receiving end of such vicious fighting tactics. God knows what else needs to be done. Don't even wanna go there!

But somehow all these tough and heroic females just as they're about to go into battle they unfortunately have this tendency to fall pregnant.

6/4/11 {and with the Gillard government seemingly determined to open up the military to women you have to ask is this really all about getting young women out and onto the frontlines of a military occupation or about getting certain females up into the high ranks of administration and management? And if a result is to make our military more 'female friendly' at what cost to the soldiery on the ground? Will this amount to a sort of dumbing down or achievement low orientation where elite male soldiery will be either ignored or left out in the cold, underutilized, probably deliberately under trained so these new female recruits can appear up to scratch? At the expense of core military units that in times of war are the ones with the professional skills and training a nation depends upon to do the initial bloody hard stuff. There's nothing wrong with females in the military but not at the expense of a proficient and effective fighting capability.

In fact, in times of War and if the professional ranks are destroyed when worst comes to worst any individual with a gun and a little gut's is usually brought into a fighting capacity even if they be young old or female, but that's something nobody wants to have to resort to-in fact many a nation has been saved by its desperate and untrained conscripts. One such example would be Australia's Kokoda servicemen from WWII}. The best thing the Gillard Government could give to our armed forces and Generals is some form of higher socio-cultural-political intelligence/awareness i.e., like not being used by bad politicians for bad wars, then getting maimed and killed & spending the rest of their lives with a grudge because of the way they were used to harass & kill innocent civilians in some far-off foreign land.

Give them the good sense to know when they are being misused, realize it and to then just say NO [our soldiers have the right. It is in the constitution].

Let's face it Lady CEO's and upper income professional females are put there by men, & more often than not choose to make their marriages with men of means even when they are well off economically themselves.

Have total respect for business women that got there of their own steam without all this government affirmative action and interference. Undeniably females must strive to be as informed and educated and as equated with the subject of politics and other fields of knowledge like the humanities the science's, economics etc., but just not with affirmative action driven easy access forms of aid that make them complacent and basically driven and facile. No one would want things to go back to the way things were in Australia prior to the 1970's when females were largely dull, uninformed and economically subservient to even more dumber blokes.

...and besides do countries like the US and elsewhere that have a prevalence of female appointees in high office positions prove to be any less amoral or vicious as countries considered less female-centric? One would have to say definitely not.

Obama not Hillary. She for one wanted to go in and bomb Iran did she not? [and Look at Thatcher]. Females are far more prone than males to problems of greed and making wars on other people so as to accumulate gold mines or diamonds and pearls and other person's real estate, are'nt they now. History is littered with em. American women of course could easily be classified as the venalest of any nations, which was why Australian females were always much coveted by both American, Englishmen and Europeans once. Not so sure these days.

It is a well-researched fact that females with higher tertiary educations DO not want to marry lower. [They often decide a relationship with another female of similar economic status is best practice]. When these become better educated and their role becomes higher paid than the man's, these generally dump their lower income male partner. Males on the reverse if these marry-down, do not dump their lower relationship partner. If these marry equal, similar. If feminism is ever going to have real relevance to the rest of the population instead of just this undefined new form of lesbianism, the roles between the two will have to be adjusted far more so than in the way they have. ie., -males still being given primary responsibility in whole host of inter-related socially driven as well economic ways, while females seem to hog all the newly realized freedoms without sharing the same responsibility's.

In essence there are Two kinds of feminists; those that see males purely from an economic perspective, and those that think all men are stupid and redundant-usually as result of direct hereditary experience ie., raised from distinctly alpha-male/capitalist 'greed is good' backgrounds or its direct apposite, that of a nature inclined toward being both pathetic and neutered. Both types suffer from the unfortunate fate of having little if any real capacity for creative thought or even common logic.

That sort of philosophical outlook should change.

Many of these wannabe new Australian style of educated and careerist 'power feministas' seem in fact to be fuelled by a sort of Presbyterian/Calvinist shop-keeping middleclass stinginess to them, in that contrary to being open and inclusive about changing the world these are not un-alike some of their more established alpha-male executive counterparts in the mining industry actually. In that they can be graspy & mean and full of bravado about how their profiteering is for the benefit of all Australians.

Australian universities also are in the main populated by a predominance of females from largely comfortable middleclass backgrounds [from a diverse array of cultural and racial perspectives] having basically enjoyed complacency most of their lives and that seem to strongly associate themselves with roles of a heightened and puritanical excessiveness esp., toward those from less salubrious backgrounds.

This is where so much of the nanny state mentality derives from-ie., highly educated middleclass woman that have a much disguised malevolence toward the lower classes. [Hence the problem with modern Labor Party politics].

Having throughout much of the 80's into early part of the 90's been a sort of roving mural artist/sign writer [admittedly was overly tempted into persuading shop owners that a more adventurous 'fine artsy' style was needed instead of the more commonly accepted purely commercial type of signwriting graphics that was then common-place] in various parts of the land one big problem you often faced was obtaining monies from the female member of the business partnership one did work for. Everything was ok up until the husbands' wife came into play and decided she wanted to control the purse strings-then trouble-and usually in a few cases bad trouble. For everyone.

Whereas with a business woman on her own, her lack of complacency and personal levels of self-gained intelligence was more prone toward positive more productive outcomes. It was about complacency levels basically.

Something that many of these feminists lack i.e. not complacency but the lack of.

Which is another reason why I think many of the wrong females [as well more than a few of the white bread nerdy & conceited looking 'boys' that seem to predominate higher educational spheres] are being put through university. The aim should be all about the education and elevation of those lesser empowered.

You also get glimpses of this mental complacency or 'role ownership' from more than a few of the many women that makeup our local library staff esp., here in Perth well used to female-centric career roles where males [especially working class hetero-sexual ones] are generally seen as being in-appropriately suited to or not necessarily allowed entry for reasons dependent on social registry or physical/mental aptitude. Campy and somewhat bitchy & sleight wristed male librarians may apply however especially if they get edgy when you have a semi-naked female in a bikini on your computer screen, now semi-naked gay looking blokes that's another story, its politically correct and therefore probably deemed excusable.

It is often quite surprising how some of these can have worked in the same position for a life time yet still are remarkably un-acquainted with various machinations and demands that are entailed with the job.

The plush new Mosman Park-Cottesloe library is run under the auspices of a lady librarian that march's up and down its long corridors of book shelves in pumps and tight skirts wearing her long greying hair in pony-tail style or when she's feeling extra glamourous she has it flowing like it used to back in 1969.

She magnifies her supposed feminist credentials by the wearing of black horn rimmed glasses not unalike Dame Edna. Meanwhile the library has become a circus full of noise and not unused to ignorant louts with misbehaving

112

little vandals for kids that when one asks them to calm down the stupid mother and the more ignorant father become enraged about the fact little kids need to be regulated.

Not by flaying them with a poker stick or slapping them round [this type of child abuse turns children into ignorant anti-intellectual adult boars or vandals that have little to no intuition or relationship with the more creative areas of reasoning and poetry, they grow up fearful, arrogant, angry or worse] but at least with harsh words and discipline if they get out of control [god how the nuns and brothers of St. Marys used to give it to us if we were naughty]. Some of these mothers are completely blissfully ignorant to this fact these days and almost arrogantly assume their children should be allowed to run amuck while they quietly and reproachfully watch them do their thing-

that is provoke and annoy others and some of the worst of them are staunchly 'assertively' white middleclass post-feminist women in their 20's and 30's [I emphasise the word assertively because more frequently than not it is this type of personality that has the most to gain from all the equal opportunity and rights campaigns that have become predominant throughout the western world over the last few decades-aggressive overly assertive personality's].

 Have even witnessed one fully grown young man not unlike a young Obama but more solidly built in big workers boots aggressively run straight at me full sprint mode down one of its corridors, like he was practising for the Olympics, swear to god he may have reached speeds of up to 15-20kms per hour [I came close to swiping him]. So many people that used to frequent this library now do not chose to come here anymore, because as wonderful as the new building is and as blessed with lots frilly nick-nacks and computer games, giant television screens, vast book shelves, children's play areas etc., etc., it has become a circus and little witchy poo in the pumps does nothing about it because she, like so many of her fellows are all look and no substance. They are little more than poseurs.

And should stress here that there is nothing wrong with sweet little kids loving library's and even having some fun with the occasional squeal of laughter, the interaction can be great. [20/9/11-witchy poo of late seems to have toned down her dress sense, gone are the Edna Everidge glass frames, as well she's not here so much anymore thank god. Still have to put up with all the instigated rubbish from the various feminist and multi-cultural lobby's groups with their little agendas though! Forever trying to turn me into a nice person]

Another careerist option that seems to demand only a females intellectual precision/perspective is the medical-nursing professions, which in the last few years seems to have become absolutely inculcated with mainly white Anglo 'feminist' professionals from the gentrified middle-classes that seem to be acutely aware of all the evils of man-kind, this alongside a mentality of almost fascistic disregard for male patients or thoughts that maybe males actually have an awareness or process of the mind that allows them feeling of some sort. This could even be described as being a kind of man-hatred. Sir Charles Gairdner and Hollywood hospitals are two such examples and i would advise any who happen to fall ill stay away from these twin festering wounds of female entrenchment.

They are infiltrated with wannabe feminist man-haters and those in their 30's 40's and older can be some of the worst. Whatever you do drag yourself and whatever ails you back out onto the streets and die if you have to just don't let the vindictives that stalk their corridors get their mitten's on you that is if you happen to be male. The female nurses from India and elsewhere friendly enough not necessarily the males these can suffer from a touch of the royal prince-highness-ness in temperament associated with coming from higher caste Indian society, even displaying at times a tendency toward creepy racial-ness. It's mainly the Anglo female. They've often been poisoned by all the feminism rhetoric. [Not to deny having experienced the occasional run-in with some fairly skanky natured Indian females over the years who somehow sought an advantage in determinedly, self-righteously proclaiming all white Australians as racist].

And more than a few of the white male doctors come with temperaments acutely activist in manner, seemingly unaware that in ways this is just another form of prejudice only encased in the cloak of virtuousness. And some of the worst of them are highly prone to racial and social agendas, in which these can tend to view white hetero-sexual males from 'gentile' backgrounds very much in the negative.

In fact, it can be so hard to find a Doctor or medical professional that won't talk down to you so eager are they to give you their bill. In fact, some of the younger ones [in their 30's & usually of white Caucasian male stock -also being very aware of their own class hierarchy] come across frequently as little more than shoddy used car salesmen and do they get miffed if you don't buy what they got to sell. You sense that they would operate on you in a hot second if they thought it would help mitigate their obtaining the latest version of a Mercedes Coupe' any quicker.

There are those of certain racial make-ups that have a quiet formidable smugness about them such as the Chinese/Asiatic female that complacently and conveniently assume their racial profile will eventually usurp that of the Caucasian race throughout most of western society and esp., Australia in the coming few decades, due mainly to the massive over-population levels of China and the South-East Asian region and there is little that can be done about it.

Multi-Culturalism is not only a great way to experience a wide variety of international food choices and customer base, it can also be a fun way for the capitalist to get cheap workers by undermining the median wages of the working population and stabilising them next to inflation and the price of consumer goods the capitalist wishes to sell or import/export. And is prone to giving the capitalist a higher opinion of his/herself than he/she should have. Multi-culturalism is brutally displacing not only the native of whatever land they emigrate toward but frequently denudes 3rd world cultures of their most productive and skilled workers.

Having been stalked now for well over two decades by the various 'multi-cultural' lobby groups [particularly from Greek, Croat, African and more recently over the last 2-3 years by those of Indian background usually with some silly white slut-ish female in tow just to teach me a lesson in race acceptance da de dah] because of my perceived insensitive views and can say now have interacted & met with many humanitarians both directly and indirectly over the decades and not one of them are on the median wage, most in fact live high off the hog of their 'multi-culturalist inter-racialist' agendas, travelling and associating only with others of their rank and nomenclature, all the while keenly celebrating their humanitarian concerns with liberal glasses of the best wines, in the best hotels, while usually owning the best real estate views too. And few of these sort of people do not come with their own underlying racism's and sexism's.

There are those of a certain political bent like the Green Party who refuse to compromise on any of their somewhat at times highly idealistic viewpoints. Not being able to associate their intransigence on certain issues as akin to fascism. Another form of complacency? Nevertheless, my intention is to still vote for these with Labor preferences in the coming election.

In the area of broadcasting complacency is exemplified by the likes of Jennifer Byrne interviewing the writer Christopher Hitchens, where she seemed determined to vilify him as a 'sexist' because he held different points of view to hers. I should emphasise here my total disinclination to support Hitchens views on the right of the Bush administration going into Iraq. Vilifying him over such views by way of supposed literary review or conversation is another thing entirely.

And while the interview conducted had an abysmal and dire lack of respect toward a writer of true talent and intelligence, it certainly highlighted the fact that this woman is a typical example of the 'girls club' form of cronyism that in the last thirty years has well and truly taken hold of not only our major independent government broadcaster [abc] but has also wrapped up in its tentacles as caressed as they maybe, the liberal and literary arts.

Where instead of broaden and enlarge our view of the world these self-serving fem-fascists have decreased its overall wider contribution and even alienated one half of its true scope- that of male involvement principally lower income male involvement to being merely uninvolved and barely amused spectators at best.

The area of Arts is another female dominated profession and also another career where a male is not particularly wanted. And many of the males that do seem to be easily accepted into arts establishment politics are often as not fascistic in their nature but fascists with a heart for the feminine? The arts community is also deeply affected by emotionalist rhetoric that seems to equate all in the visual arts as humanitarians when they patently are so rarely inclined. In fact, the far majority of them are little more than the most self-centred, ill-read, poorly thought out or enunciated, opportunistic absolutists, more often than not. Who love to be associated with humanitarian-ist objectives if they think it's going to be good for their visual art career. I've personally had more than enough serious hard headed run-ins and disputes with these type of folk because they did not like my independence or the way I possibly ran against their rules and dominions.

When the best artists are rarely involved in the pursuit of these type of agendas and usually because of their particular bent are often pushed out of the arts by politics & careerists.

This sort of complacency is everywhere in the art fraternity and the sooner they get over it the better.

Personally I'd love to see more working class single Mum's with 2 kids or more, that's spent a lift-time in the work force get the opportunity to be payed to go back to university and become doctor solicitor architect lawyer whatever. It would be good for everyone. But to be realistic there are those that do nothing more than bitch and complain about their lot and these will never have the aptitude to go higher because of their 'attitude'.

Attitude is everything.

And besides even when these do get the opportunity the system now is so skewered toward a feminist perspective these come out with the same ol' Nazi feminist attitude. The establishment has long been in the throes of-'the anti-hetero anti-male heroics going up against this great male bastion of prejudice'. That is the establishment.

Another consideration is these professional upper-middle class feminis-tas that want every female to work have obviously never experienced life on the front line i.e., lower income jobs where women are forced to take these jobs out of need, not because they necessarily enjoy it or feel having a job enhances and asserts their feminine independence. And working class males need more than groups of other males bonding with each other as compensation for being usurped of their traditional roles by being forced to take lower income labour or martial forms of subservience. [Although there are definitely 'blokey' misogynists out there that no doubt finds that sort of familiarity between other males quite comforting- also an aspect to Muslim cultures I find a little worrying frankly].

In essence Financially well off modern Females must be coerced through social guilt or government policy to provide for a male especially if he is the type of male highly intelligent but from lower economic status, with weekly monies to basically live a more socially healthy less frugal or deprived lifestyle.

Gambling, prostitutes, travel, creative study and making art such as poetry paintings sculpture and scientific/mathematic calculation, staying physically healthy-swimming, boxing, bodybuilding, weightlifting, sprinting, whatever, [typically a male's domain], must surely be a holistic and necessary part of this new policy through taxing of all these privileged and potentially privileged females of the future that want to control government, business and whatever. They cannot continue to have it all their own way.

Under no circumstances however will any intelligent reasonable minded hetero-sexual male ever really want to bed down with a two-faced manipulative un-personable self-serving skank. No matter how much money she has in her bank account or how much she has achieved in her career orientation. Simple fact, hetero-sexual males like accessible, easy natured, friendly preferably physically attractive females. If they got brains its ok. But whether they be stupid or intelligent -Self-serving, manipulation does not have to enter the equation.

The whole underlying premise of this is the fact many of these supposed 'feminists' are really using race and misogyny as reason and explanation for them to be allowed to rise to the top of the heap, when really most are deeply fundamentally orthodox wowsers and prudes & social conservatives in disguise. Not in any way at all interested in furthering intelligence, cultural enlightenment or liberal debate unless this amounts to their own gain. My basic conclusion females trying to dumb westernised white males down and make saps out of them only make them more cunning in their misogyny and supposed sexism's.

Because of the two sexes Man is greatest in both intelligence and physical ability. Though at his worst man is nasty sub-human and often mastered by those of the fairer sex.

Chapter16 Censorship Equates with Philistine Ignorance [2007]

Australia has of recent times seen a very good artist and photographer by the name of Bill Henson have his works removed from a gallery site, then be given a court order on charges of dealing indecently with minors...The case was thrown out however. There was big 'hoo-haa!' over the whole thing and the controversy continues. Even our newly elected PM Kevin Rudd came out with the statement..."He'd never seen such disgraceful art work in all his life and was sick of all these pederasts parading as artists". Confirming himself as just another goofy, philistine, Australian Prime Minister, something this country should be well used to by now.

Bit over the top for an elected Head of State considering only a few months previous he had gotten himself thrown out of a New York nightclub for a case of over-infatuation with one of its dancing girls brassiere' [pants most likely down round his ankles]. Was amazing, but it actually happened.

Not before however on being escorted out, did he close-in with a rather vicious elbow to the side of the head of one of his unfamiliar minders [the nightclubs bouncers], closely followed by a slap that sent another minder reeling sideways, and a gold tooth quivering through the air at velocity's unregistered but at least 800 metres per sec., it could very easily have pierced through flesh but fortunately did not. Instead it went glancing off the side of a customer's drinking glass before imbedding itself into one of the nightclub walls.

This was prior to being flung down the steps and out onto the street rather too heavy-handedly it might be said by some very over-enthusiastic and fairly ignorant heavy's. He was then piled on top off by two or three of these assailants/menaces' without the slightest concern as to his status as visiting foreign statesman and whether this should be accorded with a little respect. Who knows reasons for his being there may well have had to do with value-adding some of the Meter Maids back home on the

Gold Coast. Uncommon as that would be for a country like Australia. Value-adding I mean, not Meter Maids. Things only went from bad to worse thereafter, and the whole ugly mess very quickly deteriorated into an open and free-for-all fracas, in which the Prime Minister's own minders then assailed of themselves upon the nightclub bouncers in order to extricate our PM.

PM Rudd surely proved his fighting worth by biting down hard onto one of his opponent's bums in order to help assist his release from the situation.

The results of this were later to appear after the event as part of the NYC nightly news for all to see. One of the local news reporters was shown peering at an openly displayed and bloodied rear buttock, not unlike the way St Thomas and the disciples have been depicted examining the wound of Jesus in one of Carravaggio's more famous paintings, and proved the value of good, regular dental upkeep, for the marks and welts that remained were fairly regular and decidedly well incised. Incised and deep enough to have broken skin in fact. Later on giving cause for this particular individual or doorman to seek the assurances of tetanus injection and a few minor sutures where the skin refused to heal. An interesting first overseas encounter for our new PM from Queensland as well showing a side to him that went beyond the image of being simply a nerdish, bureaucrat. Or at least showing him as a very determined one.

I wrote an essay and have tried putting it onto various Australian websites but alas, -deleted. Below is this essay about the Henson case and how this whole madness continues to plague a culture that has history of such stupidity and how our arts intelligentsia are so incestuous and stupid in their own arts policy/politics/snobbery within our country that this kind of thing has to play out every now and then because Australians just don't get enough serious and intelligent art education esp., in comparison to sporting education and other. If there is any it has been taken over by a feel good, left-wing, mentality that sanitizes art to death:-

"Censorship equates with philistine ignorance"

The Bill Henson censorship case and some valid reasons why his works have been deleted. In terms of creative cultural output Australia has always been rather mediocre and largely because of the sentiments one reads about the Bill Henson censorship case and various affirmative postings on websites everywhere related to this subject. Basically speaking Australian culture has always been dominated by somewhat reactionary conservative small time thought processes. And this form of mentality has kept our nation in a very average state of cultural achievement in all honesty.

Invariably these sort of mentalities are committed to a foreign Head of State and can never ever see Australia as anything less than a colony of mother England and her cultural values. Even the opposing school of thought can only ever see a need to subvert this by going in direct opposition but using just as reactive an approach using the sledgehammers of Feminism, Multi-Culturalism, Racial or maybe environmentalist concerns.

For example, for Australians to get 'culture' we've tried to import it in as multi-culture. To varying degrees of success, ie., okay we've got lots different type food but have we as a nation created a truly significant Australian cuisine out of it all? All we've done is become a clone of other nation's food styles. -There's aussie -Greek, aussie -Italian, aussi- Indian, -Sri Lankan,-Vietnamese, -Chinese ,-French,-Thia,-Lebanese, -Mexican et al, the list goes on. One vast array of international food sources. Nothing that sets Australian food apart from any other nations or that is peculiarly indigenous to our own [actually probably at this point in time 2007 the most interesting cook is an indigenous fellow on sbs television who uses just that, 'indigenous flavours']. And we have made the country smaller in ways and less free as off-shoot without the great culture we were supposed to get out of it. There are now whole areas of Australia where if one is not of the correct ethnic or racial heritage it can feel as though you just do not belong.

Throughout history interaction of different cultures was really restrained and if it did occur it happened over vast periods of time [hundreds if not thousands of years] and the outcome was more than a type of fast food culture where the culture renews itself with a different nationality every few years, but really deep and valued contribution that originated into something uniquely original. Modern 'multi-culture' is just that, temporal and largely superficial.

Those of other nations that would try to describe Australia's contribution to world intelligence via the arts/sciences or politic etc., would generally disparagingly make mention of our koala bears, kangaroo's and other peculiar wildlife, 'Sydney', or maybe the Great Barrier Reef and that's about it. Rarely would they identify Australia as having significantly contributed in any way to world intelligence.

Which is patently wrong, even ignorant and stereotypical of them because on an individual basis Australians could be said to have contributed greatly to the world in whole manner of ways. Even belying the fact Australians have had many truly great artists/writers/actors/directors/inventors/scientists/educators/economists/humanitarians/political statesman, these have had to go and make careers overseas in places like the US/Britain or elsewhere, simply through lack of inherent supporting structures in this country and therefore in the end they may have contributed very little to Australia's advancement as a nation of ideas. And none of these could really be said to have developed or formulated a distinctive and truly Australian vernacular or school of thought through their particular type of activity whether it be; - art, music, literature, science, architecture. A fine example would have to be our greatest iconic structure the Sydney's opera house which was designed by the imagination of someone from Norway Joern Utzon. Australia has been fairly pedestrian in terms of its own architectural output except for having one or two interesting individual architects practicing here. No truly great Australian style or school of architectural design.

And although having the occasional Oscar winning actor Australia has a threadbare film industry at best and no discernible Australian school that could easily be labelled by others as identifiably Australian. OK a lot of it is small time and often leans toward the bizarre. Although we nearly had one in the early 70's, that had a wide visionary need to make film about big Australian ideas and stories it seems to have died. Though occasionally we make a really good movie one every ten years or so [Lantana, Getting Square, The Proposition, Chopper, Bad Boy Bubby, The Hard Word, Somersault, Wolf Creek, The Rabbit Proof Fence, Romulus My Father, Kenny, Ten Canoes, Candy, Animal Kingdom are some examples].

No distinctive and totally new Australian musical form has come about unless one excludes aboriginal music which largely evolved over a period of forty thousand years into what it is today even contemporary aboriginal artists are essentially feeding off aboriginal ancientness.

No great Australian industrial inventiveness that the rest of the world longs for. Odd how since Australia is dominated by roads and highways not one truly unique style of road vehicle has been allowed to come about that is either owned or fully developed and realized by an Australian manufacturer. You'd think by now Australia would be world leader in the manufacture & export of Australian designed cars, bikes, ocean-craft or something. But nothing much except that we export the occasional Holden Monaro into America which is after all an American corporate subsidiary and these control the success of such Australian designed innovation, usually to the detriment. There is a manufacturer in Tasmania that is renowned for his boat exports but even that is said to be going offshore in order to survive in the next few years. Even though we have as a nation been responsible for loads of creative innovation in a whole host of areas from manufacturing, industrial, science, health, artistic over the last century none of these have been supported by our governments [especially Liberal conservative governments]. Most of it has been pushed aside and the inventor/innovator has been literally forced to go off-shore in order to realize their creation and never come back!

Even the potential for home grown solar and new 'Green' industries have been dumbed down, by both Liberals and Labor. One would think this was Australia's natural advantage into new technology and the potential for massive and new export potential. Indeed no attempts at taking Australia into the space age with satellite or aerospace technology, when we nearly had one in the 1950's and we rank as one of the lowest countries in the world when it comes to speed of internet service even belying the fact we have probably the greatest take-up rate of IT technology on the planet, though poorly supported by an old and failing infrastructure that Australian Governments have been quite lax about re-building, particularly again the conservative side of Australian politics. This broadband is still yet to be fully implemented

126

that is not until about 2020 [and that's if the conservatives don't obtain power in the meantime and then put stop or in some way sabotage the potential of this to!]

Generally speaking, our Universities are average on a world scale much dominated by foreign students that come here largely through financial limitations rather than for our University's being centres of learning excellence. No great research and development capacity there, even in the foreseeable future. Without the support of Labor or the Liberals it seems.

No unique Australian flag, nor constitution nor Head of State [were much too dumb for that too it seems, we must only ever have a foreign monarch].

The one thing Australia has got that is an outcome of its own cultural origins and invention even though it may not be of an 'intellectual or artistic cultural asset' is the great game of Australian Rules football. A game essentially with hereditary roots having come from out of a cross between an aboriginal game of football and Irish Gaelic football, only the Australians have realized and made of this something that is much more exciting, more honed, indeed a much more spectacular competition. A magnificent game of sport that must surely one day be a major world game.

Though in truth the fond need for Australians to only ever express themselves solely through sport is largely a by-product of our colonialist lack of confidence in our own creative-intelligence ultimately. And that is about it unfortunately. The reason why? One could be forgiven for suspecting, is that Australia has always been under the yolk of those that absolutely refuse to envision Australia as anything less than a minor state that slinks in the shadow of Anglo-American cultural imperialism & hegemony. Only ever accommodating a population of around 10-25, millions even when this country could easily support 5x's this number of people basically because this suits the interests of a small echelon of rather rich, free-trade, mining orientated shareholder base [whose real loyalty is to a mainly foreign creed you cannot help but suspect]. Basically involved within the export of cheaply gained mineral resources as well agriculture and other low value commodity exports, enterprises that continually keep this nation in an under-grade, low, producing niche.

Which says a lot about the reaction you get from these when the term 'tax' is bandied about within their immediate vicinity, because these sort of individuals have by and large always viewed this country in terms of being their great big 'grown-up' backyard. And that's the extent of it and all it is ever going to be allowed to or be capable of achieving. A giant playground with which these can dinky toy truck, rocks, sand from their own little play area mine-site and off-load into their little play toy ships floating around in the kiddy plastic pool, from one side to another.-And just like spoilt self-centred children their vain hyper-ventilating attempts at self-justification by publicly lobbying via the media they largely own and operate all in their own defence which they have recently campaigned to do by way of a massive public promotional exercise designed to negate the proposal of a Mining tax by our new PM Rudd. And which ultimately exposed them all for what an avaricious group of 'australians' these people in reality were. If they had have just said nothing and left it up to their highly paid spin doctors, they may have come out looking far less stupid.

All who would want for something a little more sophisticated and less transient more culturally enriched and a little less like the spiteful scrutinizing village Australia has succumbed to being for many decades now are generally depicted by the right-wing media as evil/anti-Australian. This along with various so-called 'leftist' feminism whose over-wrought reactions toward males & sexuality only feed this type of fear driven, paranoia & insularity that has had a devastating effect on this countries intelligence and open-mindedness for most of the last century in terms of having and achieving some sort of grandeur of scale non-mining, commodity related that is. Even Australian feminism is just an offshoot of American feminist ideology from the 60's and 70's. It was not developed or initiated here and nothing new from these really except that they can be as voracious stupid and intolerant as some Australian men can at times be. What else from them? OK they want to be like men, but that's just the preposterousness of contemporary feminism when they forget their own unique abilities and try to second best males. Females will never be the new Leonardo Da Vinci's. Okay Germaine Greer was the exception, but we even lost her to the Brits and when she and her other highly gifted Aussie expats do come back to this country in order to enlighten it up or make a contribution they often sound lost and out of touch, as though they were still conversing to a nation and an era they left back in the 60's sadly. And it is such a shame their potential genius has been in the main allowed to impact other cultures but not so much the nation of their birth.

But I do not believe innovation per se it is in the female genetic makeup. The need to push the boundaries and even go to extremes is really a manly pursuit. Females have an inbuilt protective mechanism for real practical reasons. Child-birthing and Maternalism are the very antithesis of independent, individualistic, creative reasoning which is why females do certain things far better than males.

Be conservative and very organised and seek the safe option [e.g., women do well in positions of organisation, and even in certain kinds of managerial roles] but unless they are of the type of female that is abnormally masculine of character with a really unmaterialistic, irresponsible, push the envelope, take risks attitude, hard-core feminism just is not best practice for most unfortunately [the Germaine's of the world are the exception]. And the outcome is all of these reactive moralistic mental police. Full of the best of intentions but utterly lacking in liberality or imaginative scope.'

see older essay 'state of the arts'

N.B.; re- The philistines were actually a tribe or race from the Gaza region of the Sinai approx. 3000 years ago and contrary to being ignorant these were in fact far ahead of anyone else esp., in terms of metallurgy, having a monopoly over the use of industrial metals and iron, which was probably why these beat King David of the Jews in warfare. They were also more advanced than any other in areas that related to the decorative arts such as pottery.

#As of 2014 some of the things stated here no longer apply, such as our universities being mediocre-it seems they are now world's best practice or at least in the top 20. Our movie industry of late is getting more relevant and out television is changing for the better with much more local content being made and exported! PM Rudd is no longer in power and indeed the conservatives are back under Abbott.

Chapter17 "Madame Typhoon" [2018]

Only a few days gone while at a public library in a leafy-green, gentrified aspect of Perth's western 'burbs, a locale not too distant from the fair sea-breezes that often flow in from the ocean to bring about their cooling actions. Fresh saintly sea breeze greatly appreciated by the residents of this city in the height of summer. Although in winter this breeze fondly referred to as the 'fremantle doctor,' either dies or becomes impossibly blustery. It is no less than a fine, sweet familiar breath of summers that instead of doing what climate change alarmists forewarned were going to become inhospitable summers that would be capable of burning the felt hat from off all your lowly, sinful scalps.

But -No, what it has indeed done is actually make this great spread-eagled city by the sea-shore these days far milder in its climate in comparison to what was once a more common feature of this the most isolated city in the world. Once it tended toward a more wholesome full-blooded kind of summer heat which whatever it lacked in humidity, certainly made up for it in pure, sintering hellish burn, so thanks be to that climate-change alarmists everywhere.

Any how, to proceed onwards with my story of misery & woe, seated all alone as I was within the library precincts, 'the quiet room' actually when in comes a rather dithering, anguished woman of Asian extraction, quite possibly Chinese origins but doubtlessly from a long time ago, certainly she was not of a Chinese nationalist disposition from what one can tell by her very distinct broad 'aussie' vernacular. I know her mainly by sight and limited conversation. My thoughts on her are that she and associates have been quite possibly prone to stalking me over a period of months if not years? I may be wrong.

As stated, I was in fact seated by myself in this quiet space of the studious, a place where only myself and the computers were to be seen marshalled all together in semi-circular format for those who wish to work in private without the noise and clamour usually associated with modern libraries. Quiet that is...until the typhoon decided to make her appearance, whereby she felt a need to impose her ancientness, her racial & moral perfection indeed rectitude upon this undeserving heathen, this one of those Anglo-Australian males in all of her hustle, bustle & sighing sort of way!

So, in she comes whereby for an uninterrupted, 20-minute filled spree she makes out like an Asian-typhoon. Replacing this room's former peace with a newly arrived cacophony much brought about from the angry, slamming down of hand-bag against computer, including the throwing of various implements from within said bag down onto table-top as noisily as possible. Banging sounds absolutely designed to terrorize or at very least antagonize.

 Like the way she tore open each page of the newspaper she now began to read letting me know of her displeasure no doubt, and here's poor old me thinking this was a room for computer users who preferred a small measure of quiet. After all, there is a whole room devoted to those beings of the newspaper elsewhere. And a very large space it is too, hardly ever used. And so with each turn of the newspaper this capricious typhoon was seemingly determined to make a resounding 'tear open each page' as proof she was mad as hell and was not going to take it anymore. I thought Asians were supposed to be politer, considerate, quiet and gentler than us deplorable white Caucasians? Was I lied too.

Anyway after putting up with this nonsense for a quarter of an hour or more I decided to make a little of my own noise, by taking out my mobile phone and talking into it as hint-hint? 'Let's see how she likes it', I thought to myself hmmm? Nope, she definitely did not. And just like the self-entitled, hypocritical little Asiatic haranguer she truly was, she goes absolutely berserk. "YOU CANNOT USE YOUR MOBILE PHONE IN HERE!!!" she screeches.

I suggest to her that I was attempting to give her a hint to be a little less disruptive and more respectful of others peace and quiet, after all this was a quiet-room. NO!! She refuses to listen to anybody bar the activist, progressive, angry little tyrant thundering about inside of her small fierce, malevolent little mind, not unlike an Asian tyrant. Again she yells at me, "YOU CANNOT USE YOUR FUCKING FUCKING BLOODY MOBILE PHONE IN HERE YOU WHITE MALE FUCKING PIG BLAH BLAH!

Only now she is practically hysterical and utterly incommunicative in tone, a total child in adult form who is intent upon making a scene. It goes on and on, "YOU FUCKING RACIST WHITE MALE PIG. YOU MIDDLE-AGED ANGRY WHITE MALE IN A MIDDLE-AGED CRISIS. YOU FUCKING STALKER [stalker is it now?] YOU FUCKING RACIST THIS, YOU FUCKING RACIST THAT, WHO CANNOT READ THE SIGN −NO MOBILE PHONES IN HERE!!!!"

As stated this woman and various alliances of hers have had me on their calling cards for a while now seemingly knowing when I choose to do work here on various manuscripts that I maybe editing and being sure to also make an appearance themselves just to keep me company or some such? Only a week or two earlier, while working on a manuscript some helpers of the disabled decided to seat diagonally across from myself, a very unfortunate but also highly disruptive Asian guy with serious mental issues. Issues, that were in my honest opinion way too severe to have to deal with and work on one's manuscript at the same time. He immediately went into a kind of banging and wailing epiphany while gnashing his fists upon our table, until I decided I could not put up with this anymore and so I abruptly got up from the table to just go and do my work elsewhere. Unfortunately, this unfortunate man's helpers may have witnessed my immediate departure as the ruse of one deeply intolerant of the mentally ill. Fully expecting me to sit peacefully with a big smile upon my saintly brow, not un-alike the godly demeanour of a Jesus.

Nevertheless the world it seems is now run by people such as the typhoon [another of her ilk has sourced me out right as I type this little essay on first world problems and has just gone into giggling mode, clattering upon the table her computers mouse a rather pissed look to her expression an expression no doubt attributed to this bad author who offends with the writing of 'misery literature' that is, when it is not filled with his sexual ly explicit goings-on and other merry sort of corruptions].

And a monster Madame Typhoon indeed was, a sad lonely monster I suspect although admittedly a monster in the form of a not unattractive woman of at least fifty or so years, who must have once been quite the dish. I think somehow the years have made her far too cynical however, no doubt in part because of poor emotional-intelligence? Something which a lot of these activist-progressive sorts do seem to suffer a real lack thereof, that and some quite uninformed views relating to literature, art, philosophy, politics or in other words, a great lack of good reading. Conformational bias is usually the outcome and a reason why so many remain categorically stuck with either a left or right political perspective. Forever to remain thus inclined amen.

Madame Typhoon's problem in all likelihood stemmed from the fact her ancestry was Chinese but a little Chinese perfect too perhaps? Expecting others to imbibe such fine notions too, though in truth even the Japanese who are rather xenophobic themselves greatly feared the Chinese form of insularity as even superior to their own kind, which was surely the reason why they attempted to take them out in the second world war.

The world is now full of these first world activists often with first world anger management issues who all wanna play at being hard done-by. Then they go home to their neat and well tendered gardens or cafes to calm down and act all civilized, well at least passive-aggressively civilized unless of course their café-latte or mocha-latte fails to be served-up and placed precisely where they directed it to be put, just a little to the left or right of the crisp, white napkin beside the miniature pastel-coloured, flower-pot. Don't you dare put it just a millimetre out or all hell will break loose! Maybe hard physical work is their one true companion or maybe they could all join the army. Then come back and gripe about white male pigs getting it far too easy. Join the army, get a gun and go to Afghanistan all you fine hardy ladies of the progressive passive-aggressive left.

Including you Madame Typhoon you with the passive-aggressive need to ask people to put on their shoes because your heightened senses cannot deal with other people's foot smell as you protect yourself by putting on your big duffle-coat as way of showing your concern at the diabolical intentions of males around type-writers. And while you're at it Madame Typhoon you could hone-up on a little worldly history and especially history related to the first voyages of Europeans into the heart of china, well the edges of it really round-eye was never welcomed into its heart only its edges. Or, the dismissive manner with which they and their newly created technological achievements encountered by an ageing empire greatly smug in its own at such a time vast cultural, technological [and doubtlessly racial] accomplishments and have been for a very long time since. Well certainly up until a few short decades ago.

Because it does seem to some that the Chinese are very determined to make the world into a second reconquest, a second great China realm of Empire. Largely it has to be said, by way of stealing any and all of other people's intellectual patents and innovations to be stealthily claimed all for the greater good of China. Originality largely bought and paid for by the western taxpayer not the Chinese one. And hauling it all of back into the heartland of the dragon. This new empire of the dragon we must all one day abide by, or else it's the 're-education' centre for you my un-conformist but merry friend, I somehow doubt will ever achieve such an agenda. Chinese ethnocentrism can be based too much on copying others hard won innovations. To be original one must have a degree of human rights. And, to be honest I do not see many round-eye towns anywhere across Asia, any less China. All one see's is the white westerner being invited into Asia/china only as mere tourists. Hence, they must abide by the Asian, the African or mid-eastern/Arab way IF they bring money into the orient or Africa or wherever they go that is not of their own particular culture or racial make-up. You can spend just do not ever try taking it out by way of work or investment or business practices.

Across the western world however, there a gazillion-million China-towns, or Vietnam towns or Thai- towns, whatever towns. Free to make trade. To live. To work. To marry and have same rights of citizenship. To safely harbour money, investments and a company's intellectual rights of ownership.

It's such a pity Madame Typhoon is too lamentably self-consumed and racially confirmed to stop calling others out over their perceived racism's. One could also make mention of Tibet-the Uigar people-china's other indigenous peoples-working class servitude & slavery-over fishing-Spratley Islands-Hong Kong et al.

End.

www.ingramcontent.com/pod-product-compliance
Lightning Source LLC
Chambersburg PA
CBHW070356290526
45790CB00004B/1521